DISRUPTION OUT OF A BOX!
An Entrepreneur's Guide to Success

KEITH HERMAN

A Nimitta Book

Keith Publishing

Los Angeles, CA

Copyright © 2020 Keith Herman

All rights reserved. This book may not be reproduced in whole or in part, or transmitted in any form, without written permission from the publisher, except by a reviewer who may quote brief passages in a review. Nor may any part of this book be reproduced, stored in a retrieval system, or transmitted in any form or by any means graphic, electronic, mechanical, photocopying, recording, or other, without written permission from the publisher.

This edition published by Keith Publishing
For information address Keith Publishing, Los Angeles, CA

First Edition
ISBN: 978-1-7348232-8-8
Library of Congress Control Number: 2020905706

For information about special discounts for bulk purchases, please contact Keith Publishing at business@keithherman.com.

Cover Design by Visualarts
Text & Layout Design by eacodes

Printed in the United States of America
10 9 8 7 6 5 4 3 2 1

DISRUPTION OUT OF A BOX!
An Entrepreneur's Guide to Success

Contents

Acknowledgments VII

Dedication IX

Introduction XI

CHAPTER 1: The Biggest Lesson 1

CHAPTER 2: The Makings of an Entrepreneur 15

CHAPTER 3: The Rise & Fall 25

CHAPTER 4: The Bittersweet Taste of Failure 33

CHAPTER 5: Eureka 41

CHAPTER 6: Where's Dinner 49

CHAPTER 7: The Greatest Hurdle 59

CHAPTER 8: The Perfect View 71

CHAPTER 9: Meet My Boyfriend 77

CHAPTER 10: The Beauty of Technology 95

CHAPTER 11: Comedy Central 105

CHAPTER 12: Off to the Races 127

CHAPTER 13: The End of the Line 147

CHAPTER 14: Mystic Money 155

CHAPTER 15: Mapping & Mastering Your Success 161

CHAPTER 16: Conclusion 173

Acknowledgments

Thank you to my friends, colleagues, and acquaintances for incessantly prodding me over many years to share my experiences in a book.

A big thanks to Beck, my homie, for keeping me accountable for completing the book.

To Brad for being so supportive and for providing the perfect hideaway.

Most of all, thank you to Justin, Zach & Tess. My life has and always will be most rewarding because of your illumination. I am forever grateful!

Dedication

I dedicate this book to all the people with a dream, considering taking the journey, and all the risks associated with the tasks to realize it. In the business world, we call these people entrepreneurs if they commence the journey.

> Sometimes the road less traveled is less traveled for a reason.
> JERRY SEINFELD

Have you ever wanted to do something and changed your mind almost immediately because either self-doubt or fear overcame you? Perhaps you wanted to learn how to play an instrument and never even picked it up because you thought to yourself, "I'll never learn how to play it, and even if I do, I won't be any good at it, so why even waste my time?" Sound familiar? Or perhaps, in the case of speaking in front of an audience regardless of how big or small? Or, even talking to a stranger that you find attractive or looks interesting?

On the flip side, have you ever been overwhelmed with the desire to do something? So much so, that nothing could stop you? Perhaps take a trip to a destination you've always dreamed about or challenge yourself to accomplish something or make a late evening run for pizza or ice cream. Of course, you have!

Perhaps this book will present the opportunity to see things differently. Possibly self-doubt and fear will become irrelevant? Maybe you will choose to live in the realm of possibilities and not just probabilities? Maybe, residing among the options, life will become more enjoyable, exciting, and meaningful in many ways? Perhaps you are ready to take the plunge?

Perhaps your time is now?

Introduction

I DECIDED TO WRITE this book to share with others the things I have learned, which have led to enormous profits and, at the same time, expanded and enriched my experience, enjoyment, and appreciation for life.

I do not consider myself an expert as others insist; instead, I see myself as an engaged student of life. I continue to explore and educate myself on the things that matter and follow the things that time and time again prove to be true.

In the face of constant inquiry on how I repeatedly achieved successes, I needed to seriously take considerable time to reflect before producing this book for others to consider. Hopefully, it will be used as a workbook to assist you in your quest for success.

Candidly, I have had more challenges than you can imagine, yet, through trial, error, research, and the shared wisdom of countless others, it is undeniable there is a clear path to financial and personal success as well as happiness. May this book lead you to yours.

CHAPTER 1

The Biggest Lesson

IT WAS A MAGNIFICENT summer evening in Los Angeles. A perfect 80 degrees, dry, breezy, and absent of clouds. People were out on the town, milling about energetically, smiling, laughing, and enjoying the trendy shops on Melrose, the restaurants from Hollywood to Santa Monica to the Valley, newly released movies, shows, concerts, comedy clubs, the stars from the Griffith Park Observatory and more. Magic was most certainly in the air! But how would I know?

I could feel a twitch, a jolt, and the broadening pressure between my right side ribs about mid armlength's down. I suddenly snapped to attention as my classmate's elbow eased off my ribcage. "Wake up, man!" said Jim with a deadpan face. Jim was a good buddy of mine at the time and always had everyone's best interest at heart. I felt like I had let him down. I looked up and saw the professor lecturing away behind the podium at the front of the expansive moderately lit theater shaped auditorium. I thought to myself, "what the hell am I doing here? I've got the creeps, and this guy and this place are giving it to me!" In that exact instant, Jim spoke softly, "Keith, you can't continue working full-time and going to school full time. It's just not possible, something's gotta give!"

It was telepathy! I could feel the chills run down my back, my arms straight to my fingers. The reality of the situation was more chilling and sobering than telepathy. Jim could not have been any more precise! I quietly and unassumingly slid my books into my backpack and nonchalantly exited.

I drove home without thinking, walked through the front door, knocked off my shoes onto the rust shag carpeting, and planted myself on the tan and burnt orange hand-woven cotton couch sprawled out with my feet extended onto the thick hand-carved oak wood coffee table. I stared at the blank TV screen as if to find an answer, but it was absent. I shared the apartment with my sister, and the lack of incense burning reminded me she must be out and about. It was entirely silent; it was necessary, the hours needed to pass with angst and sullenness.

I couldn't avoid the obvious a wink longer. I had run out of hiding places, and it was time to face the music. I knew I needed to pursue something else, something that wholly set my stomach ablaze, something that would keep me awake at night with exhilaration regardless of the risks. Instead, I was a zombie! I was numb, unconscious, checked out, and didn't even realize how miserable and unhappy I had been. Worst of all, I knew the truth. My life was slipping away with every moment I sat there. I became nauseous, incapacitated, and felt destitute. I was lost, clueless, and scared. I had to take action! I needed to move, do something, or possibly feel death.

For as long as I can recall, as a child growing up, I was prodded regularly to get an advanced degree. Become a doctor, a lawyer, an architect, or anything with an advanced degree so you will always have a sweet life and something to fall back on if things get rough. My father referred to it as "a ticket," and I was about to tear mine up.

It wasn't just a sign of the times; It was my father who never went to college. He had left his home at the age of thirteen and grew up on his own. Along his way, he ended up in the Marines during the Korean War, where he advanced to drill sergeant. He managed to remain at Paris Island and networked his way through managing all the food for the officers that kept him from getting deployed. He then went on to open a bakery and eventually expanded until he built the largest donut manufacturing facility in existence at the time. Located in Brooklyn, New York, I frequented it often in the middle of the night to watch them prepare the donuts. The would work through the night to ready them for early morning delivery to all of the stores within the subways of New York City and the major department stores in the Tri-State area, a total of 90+ stores.

When I was twelve years old, my father decided to exit the business to move onto another opportunity. It was one of many business ventures to follow including manufacturing electronic components & printed circuit boards, a few microfilm businesses, acquiring distressed companies with hard assets and liquidating them along with a handful of his inventions, and so on, all the while continuing to preach to me about getting my "ticket." At times when he felt I wasn't listening to his advice, he found it cute to remind me of the difference between life and an erection. "Life is Always Hard!"

I now found myself looking squarely in the face of my worst fear. My thoughts were in direct conflict with the "get a ticket" brainwashing. The pressure was overwhelming, but I couldn't go another minute. And, so, I simply surrendered.

It was as if a weight immediately lifted off my chest. I could only now breathe even though I had nothing, no savings, and now no job since the job was predicated upon me finishing school, no plan, not even an idea. "What the f.... am I going to do now?"

I sat in solitude for a couple of days as I repeatedly told myself to remain calm. It was almost like a continual religious chant to program myself to get beyond the confusion, the conflict, and the pain. Everyone around me was in disbelief and just as confused. I couldn't take anyone's call and just watched the phone as it would ring. Through it all, I was able to maintain a sense of peace and balance. Eventually, the thought crossed my mind, "what if I forget about getting an advanced degree? What if I don't become a doctor, a lawyer, an architect, or anything with an advanced degree? What if advanced degrees don't even exist, what then?"

BOOM! Lightning struck! I finally had an original thought. In that moment of asking the question, I realized, "what if I change my perspective?" And, as I allowed it to happen, immediately, all sorts of possibilities flooded my mind faster than I could process them. That moment was a defining moment for me! I learned two valuable lessons that would stick with me to this very day. First, there is always more than one way to view things. Second, when we are open our minds to other points of view, more possibilities and potential outcomes exist. These two lessons set the stage for countless new opportunities and invaluable experiences. Because, as my perspective changed, my thoughts changed, and so did my future.

Among those first experiences was a re-introduction to reading. To that point, my entire life was fraught with the drudgery of reading. It seemed as if I just never possessed the desire to read. Every book I had read up until that point had been a chore. A long and drawn-out process taking longer than I would have liked, and it seemed I regularly got very little to any useful information from it. So naturally, the initial thought of me reading more books was absurd, upsetting, distressing, frankly borderline torture. There were only a few exceptions, such as J.D. Salinger's angst and alienation themed "The Catcher in the Rye." Dalton Trumbo's anti-war novel "Johnny Got His Gun" and Ernest Hemingway's war story "A Farewell to Arms."

On the other hand, my most recent memory was of two insidious books whose names I could not purge fast enough. They were two computer programming books for a mainframe computer. If you don't know what that is, either did I. And, things didn't get much better from there.

It was the early eighties, at the University of Miami. I had signed up for what was then called an "Independent Study Program" in addition to my classes. The Independent Study Program allowed me to work on a project within a field of interest to provide a practical experience rather than just reading a book and sitting through lectures to take an exam. Of course, I'd receive credit towards my degree without even having to take a test, and I was very excited about this prospect since the traditional approach to education had proven to be monotonous and already worn me thin. I thought I had scored and somehow outsmarted my classmates with this diversion, but oh, how I was soon enlightened.

It was an exemplary, paradoxically, sunny, yet humid weekday morning in Miami. Not a cloud in the sky as I lead myself out of my apartment. I hastened to the car and off to school to meet the host of my Independent Study program. I was ridiculously intoxicated with enthusiasm as I thought of the flexibility and freedom I would have for a change. I would coast through the semester without an excessive load. I had outsmarted the system, a coup de tat!

In a blink, I was in the expansive marble and glass lobby of an otherwise bland building on campus that I had never even noticed before just waiting on him. And in he walked! Professor Jack Tapp, Dr. Jack Tapp! His name I would always remember but his face I had soon forgotten.

"Good morning! You must be Keith.", he said. "Yes, nice to meet you, Dr. Tapp.", "Come with me, and I'll show you around," he replied. We left the bright lobby and walked down a long, dimly lit corridor with doors evenly spaced on each side roughly thirty paces until he came to an abrupt stop. He leaned to his left as he dropped his head momentarily to recall where he had left his keys. He fumbled through his pockets. I was now getting nervous as an eerie feeling began to set in. "Ah, here they are!" he exclaimed and unlocked the door and proceeded in.

I followed him as he flipped on the lights. And there was my future! It was a long rectangular room filled with boxes waste high and even lined the back walls up to the ceiling. I hadn't seen so many boxes since I visited The New York City Library, where my dad had procured a contract to microfilm countless documents for preservation and space-saving purposes. The feeling was less than optimistic.

"So, Keith, this is where you'll be working for the foreseeable future. Somewhere behind all these boxes is a computer, and you'll be using it to analyze all these documents. We collected the documents from several local health fairs conducted in malls."

He then popped the lid off one of the boxes, reached in and plucked out a manila folder crammed into the box. Documents were sitting disrespectfully within this envelope, and they appeared to be various questionnaires of sorts. He took a cursory look at each of them and then buried them back into the folder, placing the folder atop the open box. Next, he maneuvered away from the carton and started to wander randomly around the room, getting in between a handful of other containers in search of something until I caught an "ah-ha there they are!"

With his back to me, I saw him leaning over some boxes as if to be reaching for something. And in fact, he did! I saw him stand upright and then whirl around with two chunky books in his left hand. Each of the books was as thick as a brick.

"You're going to need these!" he said. "I'm sorry," I replied with a look of bewilderment and disbelief. "There must be some misunderstanding here. I signed up for a project, having to do with stress and coronary heart disease. I don't know anything about computers!"

In an instant, he was chuckling, and then it soon turned to uncontrollable laughter. I stood there like a deer in the headlights waiting for some clarity! He gradually settled down and blurted, "Don't worry, Keith, you'll be fine. No one else knows how to use a computer either, and that is why I'm giving you the books. You're a smart kid, I have all the confidence you will figure this all out, and when it's all said and done, we will get to publish a paper with the results. Exciting, trust me!" And then, he was gone! No rebuttal, nothing! I just stood in astonishment with the two books as time ceased. Eventually, I came to, took the books, and left figuring I would deal with it later.

A few days passed, and I decided to call good old Jack and break the news to him that I was out. I wasn't in for his adventure, and he was going to have to find someone else. I made the call and, of course, got his answering machine. It would be days before I got a call. We finally spoke, and he told me that there was no one else that had signed up, and he knew this was a tall order, so he didn't have very high expectations. Whatever I was able to do would be of value, and I would get my credits regardless.

With nothing at stake, I figure what the hell, I've got nothing to lose. I can work at my own pace. It was the early 80s in Miami, and there were plenty of other things to keep me occupied. The books conveniently disappeared in a mess on my dining room table, and I let things slide for a few weeks until I got around to cleaning up my place.

There they lay, so on that day, I made the momentous decision to pick up the first book. It genuinely was a brick.

I mean, you could seriously hurt someone with it just by lobbing it at them. The book was a programmer's guide for the computer language called COBOL. By that time, I had already taken all sorts of advanced math courses, physics classes, and organic chemistry classes, and still, this book was intimidating. I hadn't taken a single computer class and didn't even recall them offered at the time. I had never seen a publication in my life so thick with such long pages and tiny print. There were formulas on all the pages that were hard to understand. They were outright foreign, and I had no one to consult for guidance or clarity.

I picked up the next book in hopes of something better only to find more of the same except this book was a programmer's guide to a different language called FORTRAN. I had gotten myself into a pickle this time! By this time, it was too late to change course. I needed the credits, and it was too far down the road to switch.

As history would go, I took the road less traveled, such as technology pioneers Larry Ellison and Steve Wozniak and, decided to learn what I could in the hopes of something greater. After all, I had nothing to lose.

Weeks passed and nothing from Tapp, quiet as a mouse. I thought, "this is remarkable; he doesn't even care!" It would be a few weeks more until I heard from good old Jack. "Hi Keith, how's it coming?" "Well, Dr. Tapp, I'm reading the books and trying to figure out the best way to approach this project. There are quite a few documents, as you know. They will all need to be coded, in some fashion or another, for the computer to analyze them. If you could help me make that determination, it would certainly save us quite a bit of time."

Again, nothing but a chuckle on the other end of the phone." Don't worry, Keith, I'm sure you'll figure it out." At this point, it was just funny to me, the whole situation. I clearly could see that it wasn't even possible to finish this project. Because, paradoxically, if I could figure out a way to code all the documents, I still needed to solve two significant challenges. First, which language to choose to program the computer. At this time, there was no windows or user-friendly operating system as we know today. Back then, when the computer started up, the only thing visible was a black screen with a blinking symbol such as the following:

>:

The second challenge was to figure out how to code and input all the data into the computer; it was simply impossible for me to do it on my own. The amount of data in that room, even by today's standards, was tremendous.

Nevertheless, I would press on, and before I knew it, the semester was coming to an end. It was time to face the music. I met with Dr. Tapp and explained to him the situation and how sorry I was to have been unable to complete the project. I thought it was laughable even indefensible that I hadn't done anything. And, his response?

Quintessential Jack, "Well, then I guess you'll just have to continue through the next semester so we can get this done." A big smile came over his face, followed by, "Oh, and of course, congratulations, you've earned your credits for this semester!" It was clear I wasn't getting off the train so quickly or anytime soon.

That was the last I saw of Jack. For the following year, I worked on the project routinely. I flipped a coin and chose the programming language COBOL; it was just time to do or die. I figured out a way to code all the documents using several strings or a series of numbers. I then filled out a requisition request for IBM punch cards and the authorization to hire students part-time to code the punch cards and to perform data entry. Before I knew it, I had the punch cards and enough students to get started. I was feeling somewhat relieved knowing the students would be processing the cards, which would give me time to figure out the programming for all the analyses. The students took their time combing through the documents and coding the punch cards for later use. They continued to work around the clock, and after just short of another year, they finished. It was now all up to me to deliver the critical data to get this "soon to be famous ground-breaking paper" published.

I had four weeks left to get the job done, but I still had not figured out how to program the mainframe computer. I spent those weeks locked in the now stark room that hosted just the mainframe against the wall and a work desk and chair. All the documents left to a storage facility, and it was now quite clear that everything was nearing a conclusion. With two weeks left, I finally figure out by reading that behemoth how to get the stats and hurriedly pulled the trigger!

Voila! Within a matter of minutes, the results were in! Unfortunately, the wrong conclusions. Something had gone awry, and everything was worthless. It was a year and a half of my life, and it was all for nothing. I had a week left until graduation and might not get the final credits I needed if Jack was upset. I went back through the book and realized the errors were because of improper coding of the data. It was now a matter of finding the mishaps and correcting them.

It was graduation morning, and while everyone was out on the lawn at the University of Miami anxiously awaiting the delivery of their diploma, I'm enjoying the empty computer room engrossed in a colossal book that would determine my fate. As the band played on, the faintly muffled speeches continued as I raced to get the final run of data. I could hear the benediction and screams of joy. I imagined the green and orange gowned crowd tossing their caps in the air, and in a flash, saw the beauty of technology and was grateful to be sharing the exhilarating feeling of success. The results had come in, and they were spectacular! However, my taste for reading was never quite the same!

CHAPTER 2

The Makings of an Entrepreneur

IT'S NOW QUITE A few years later, and I realize for me to overcome the challenges before me, it's going to require a whole other level of learning similar to when I had the difficulties with the Independent study project in college. It's going to need to be a broader view with greater possibilities. In other words, access more information than I was currently receiving for me to realize my dreams. And, since this was pre-internet days, the only choice was to read more books.

Old habits die hard, and my level of resistance was high, but it was time to dive. And, so I did and quickly concluded it was unequivocally in my best interest in light of the present circumstances. Candidly, I always knew in the bottom of my heart that it was the right thing to do. It was now time for me to accept the facts and to change my perspective on reading so I could glean the information I so desperately needed to succeed.

I took off to the local bookstore feeling calmer than usual, and when I arrived, just before entering, promised myself to perceive the visit as an adventure like going to the movies rather than a mandatory to visit a temple or church for a service. I perused the aisles as if I was in a hardware store, which was one of my favorite past times that spanned back to my childhood.

I eventually made my way to the self-improvement section and began to dig in. I carefully looked at every book I handled as a potential piece of gold or needle in a haystack. I circumspectly read the table of contents of each work and then flipped to the back to see how many pages there were total. After all, old habits die hard! Before I knew it, I had made my selections and headed to the register. It was those books that would forever change my perspective on reading and bestow one of the grandest impacts of my life.

One of those books was the E-Myth by Michael E. Gerber. The E-Myth had been recommended to me by an old friend and turned out to be a fantastic read for four specific reasons.

First, it was minimal in size, thin, and with large type. In other words, it was not intimidating. That was always the primary consideration for reading a book.

Second, the premise of the book centered around points of view.

Third, it restored my faith in reading. The book did deliver its message quickly, and it indeed had meaning to me.

And fourth, the book taught me that great businesses are built from the top down rather than the bottom up. In other words, you need to focus on the big picture and then architect the roadmap all the way down to the details to succeed.

The next book I read was by Steven J Fogel, one of the founders of Westwood Financial Corporation, a Los Angeles based real investment and management company. I bought this book because, at that time, I was continually noticing Westwood Financial signs around town. It seemed like Westwood Financial either managed or owned every corner shopping center located in Los Angeles. I figured this guy must be doing something right, and I want to be in real estate, so I take a crack at it. I also thought, if the book turns out to be any good, perhaps he could become a resource one day?

This book fascinated me! I found it so because it too had to do with many points of view. I remember a specific passage where Steven discussed how to purchase real estate with little to no money as a down payment, something that was of great interest to me. He explained how to evaluate your financial picture, and that included your capital resources. His approach pointed out that it is not always necessary to have cash in the bank to purchase a property. One must consider other assets.

Ah ha, once again, point of view! A viewpoint I had never seen. Steven suggested that available resources should include things such as available credit that included lines of credit, credit cards, and even people that would loan you money. The light bulb in my head went off, and I thought to myself, "this guy is a genius!" These thoughts had never even crossed my mind. And why would they? I hadn't truly entered the business world at this point. However, there was no time to waste. It was time to put this knowledge to work!

I put the book down and dialed up my best friend, Larry, on his car phone. "Where are you?" "I'm in the Sepulveda Pass headed to the Valley.", he replied "Turn around and come to my place, now!", I said. And then the usual banter went on for a few moments until I shrieked, "its urgent!" and hung up.

Larry and I grew up back in New Jersey and were inseparable; there wasn't even a scintilla of a chance that he wouldn't comply. We had shared too much history with our woven love of live music, comedy clubs, and restaurants. You see, we had burned the midnight oil and beyond countless nights staying out all night until it was time to get home to get ready for school. We would frequent venues in New Jersey and New York City to see new, upcoming, and established music acts. The locales varied from tiny hidden clubs to stadiums such as The Ritz, CBGBs, Danceteria,

The Mudd Club, Max's Kansas City, Hitsville, Madison Square Garden, and so many more. Many of the acts we saw blew up overnight and lasted for decades. They included Ramones, Patti Smith, U2, Tom Petty, The Vapors, Pink Floyd, Blondie, Beastie Boys, The Cars, Joe Jackson, B-52S, Talking Heads and on and on. We also made the rounds for laughs. The Cellar, Carolines, Catch a Rising Star, Freddy's, Dangerfield's, and more to see the likes of Richard Prior, Rodney Dangerfield, Jerry Seinfeld, Eddie Murphy, Jay Leno, Andrew Dice Clay, Chris Rock, Tim Allen, Dennis Wolfberg, Sam Kinison and more.

Larry worked for an up and coming real estate firm in Encino, California, called Marcus & Millichap at the time. I would visit him at their offices and chat with his manager Harvey and his colleagues John, Gene, Bernie, Arnie, Marty, Ron, Henry, Stephan, and a handful of others, whose names escape me. I was in school at the time, but I enjoyed being a fly on the wall as they grandstanded their stories about putting deals together and cashing big checks. The kind of bank drafts that would have me up at night wondering what I was doing. These guys were indeed a cast of characters and could have had a hit TV show long before "The Office" with Steve Carell. Larry was growing tired of the office scene, and so I was anxious to speak with him about my idea.

He arrived at my tiny third-floor one-bedroom apartment in Westwood in twenty flat and, in typical Larry fashion, buzzed the intercom to the tune "Anything" by

Dramarama. I buzzed him in and waited for him to continue Anything on the front door. He had officially arrived, and it was time to get down to business. "Come on in we need to talk.", I said, "This better be good! I was on my way to make some money.", he replied. "Oh, this is better than good I've decided to go into real estate, and we can become partners."

He went catatonic, the room went silent, and I just stared at him, waiting for him to come out of the ether. "So, how's this going work? You don't have a license!" he said. "No problem, my classes from law school transfer over and allow me to sit for the real estate exam immediately, and I can have my license in 30 days. There's just one thing I need from you." "And what's that?" he said.

And that's when Fogel kicked in, "I just need you to loan me $1500 a month until we close a deal which I'm sure will be within 60-90 days tops." He thought for a moment, a very long moment, and then said, "You got yourself a deal, but I've got to go, I need to be in the Valley I'm late." And, raced for the door. It worked! My best friend just became my best resource.

Larry and I were off to a great start and were soon rolling in the dough. We both wanted more and were dreaming big. But sadly, we had a very different dream. Our good fortune soon took its toll, and Larry accidentally passed away. I was now on my own and needed to transition.

It would be the books that would be responsible for transforming me from "Keith Herman, California Real Estate Broker" as recognized by the California Department of Corporations into Keith Herman, Real Estate Investor and Developer almost overnight and from literally nothing. Out of the realm of possibilities, I began buying and selling Real Estate Purchase Agreements instead of trying to be the broker between buyers and sellers of commercial properties. I deliberately chose this path because it gave me more control over transactions and the opportunity to make substantially more money than as a broker.

Buying and selling these Agreements became a fad during the mid to late 1980s. Real estate values were appreciating feverishly. It was unprecedented and quite an opportunity. Buying and selling the Purchase and Sale Agreements to another buyer for a fee involved far less risk with far less money. It also meant one could enter into more transactions with the same amount of cash in hand.

Property transactions at the time required a deposit that was typically 3% of the purchase price. This 3% was far less than a down payment that was generally 20% - 25% of the purchase price and made it possible to have control over the sale of the property for the duration of the Agreement. It did, however, involve some risk. The risk was you needed to get the Agreement resold before the closing or risk losing the deposit.

Because investor demand for commercial properties was so high at the time, values were rising so quickly that sometimes these Agreements were being resold more than once. In some instances, the Agreements changed hands two, three, or even four times within the timeframe of the initial Agreement.

This new strategy was a game-changer for me for several reasons. First, I had more control over the property as the owner of the Agreement versus a broker trying to get a listing or selling a property without a listing. Second, I was no longer competing with fellow real estate agents and brokers because I was now a buyer. Third, I didn't have to work as hard to find deals because now all the agents and brokers, once competitors, were now bringing me all their properties for sale for me to buy so they could collect their commissions. Fourth, my deal flow increased exponentially from all the opportunities coming in from other agents and brokers, which allowed me to close more transactions. Fifth, I was making substantially more money because I was closing more deals and for higher profits per deal. And sixth, my status in the community soared as deals closed because the brokers were collecting their commissions, and I was receiving more publicity.

It was crystal clear that all of the reading was paying off. And, the proof was in my bank account. The two books restored my faith in learning through books and gave me a greater awareness and freedom. I now was able to view things from other perspectives and have far more opportunities. It also gave me the foresight to plan the course of every one of my endeavors and investments. In other words, I realized that I had the capability and the resources available to change my perspective, create new opportunities, change my thoughts, and ultimately change my future. Yes! The future was looking very bright, until

CHAPTER 3

The Rise & Fall

FAILURE!

As quick as it came, it was gone.

I just went through the most exhilarating ride of my life in every respect imaginable and then in roughly the same amount of time slowly but surely bled out. I had gotten married to my girlfriend of seven years, was blessed with my two boys, acquired several cash-flowing apartment buildings, built a large stock and bond portfolio. I also purchased my first home, a BMW, Jeep Cherokee, many other possessions, enjoyed many vacations and all within what seemed like just a handful of years. And then, thanks to the "Savings and Loan Crisis," watched it all slip away.

Unlike the rise, the fall seemed like an eternity! It was akin to watching the final play of the Super Bowl in extra slow motion. Your team never won a Super Bowl and about to cross the goal line for the winning touchdown only to be stripped of the ball and having to watch helplessly the other team run the length of the field for a touchdown and emerge the winner.

The Savings and Loan crisis, up until that time, was the most significant collapse of banks since the Great Depression of 1929. More than 1,000 nationwide savings and loan banks failed, approximately 1/3 of all the savings and loan banks in the US. The Resolution Trust Corporation, commonly referred to as the RTC, was created to clean up the mess, and ultimately, just under 750 of those failed banks closed.

Also, more than 1,600 banks failed and were closed or received financial assistance from the Federal Deposit Insurance Corporation (FDIC). When the dust settled, approximately only half of all the federally insured savings and loans remained. The estimated total cost of the crisis by the US General Accounting was around $160 billion.

The crisis had brought the US real estate markets to an absolute grinding halt during the early 90s. Overvalued savings and loan loans went into default as builders and property owners were unable to sell or lease out their properties due to an oversupply. The properties reverted to the banks at an unprecedented rate, and values went into a free fall. Banks were not receiving income from their failed loans and could not pay their customers. They could not manage the foreclosures and had no resources to manage the properties. Worst of all, the country was in panic mode;

no buyers were willing to purchase private or foreclosed properties to create liquidity for the banks. Therefore, they collapsed, and financing disappeared.

With prices falling and no sign of bank financing for the future in sight, no one wanted to part with their money. There was no choice when it came to purchasing property other than to pay 100% cash. Initially, there were no private lenders because they had no inclination on how deep the prices would fall and were reluctant to lend. The result created a situation where the buyers dried up, and the real estate transactions came to an abrupt halt. They sat on the sidelines for a handful of years before entering the market and, even then, would only make very conservative loans on the order of fifty percent loan to value.

These were extremely challenging years for most people in one way or another. I had no previous experience with such an economic situation, and everyone around me that claimed they did was saying that it would take at least five years to turnaround. It was inconceivable and something I didn't want to face. It was a time frame that significantly exceeded my savings, and the thought horrified me. My peers were dropping like flies, and stories of their misfortune were unpleasant, at the least.

Nevertheless, I was determined to survive come hell or high water. It had now been a couple of years of working every day without making a single dollar and trying to find creative ways to make deals but to no avail. The buildings I had acquired were no longer generating cash flow because of the dramatic decline in rents. Without any income, I was slowly but surely liquidating stocks and bonds to stay afloat. I was worn as mentally thin as humanly imaginable and knew I needed help from beyond my current resources.

Once again, it was time to head off to the book store with a very tall order to find something both highly inspirational and motivational to keep up my spirits and keep me moving forward. I reluctantly purchased what seemed to be a popular choice at the time called "Awaken the Giant Within How to Take Immediate Control of Your Mental, Emotional, Physical and Financial Destiny" by Tony Robbins. Tony Robbins was as hot as could be and with good reason. Countless people like myself that needed something to turn to during this terrible period, and "Awaken the Giant Within" seemed like an excellent choice.

The book was quite intimidating. It resembled a brick, and It was over 500 pages, which was twice my usual read. Even though I learned to now appreciate books and not despise reading, I still possessed the awful habit of considering the total pages for the book and the average amount of pages per chapter to determine if I felt I could realistically finish the book. I was confident I could do it, but it seemed like it would take months, and that was not comforting.

I honestly had mixed emotions about reading this colossal book and the cost vs. the benefits. On the other hand, I needed some momentous assistance. Colossal assistance! So,

I took the book and quickly made my way to the register before changing my mind.

I committed to reading at least ten pages every day and especially more whenever I found my spirit dipping to an unmanageable low. And, as you can imagine, the lows were far more frequent than I had envisioned. It was remarkably challenging going to work day after day as I continued to go through the remainder of my savings with nothing in sight. But I was determined to finish the book and succeed in business no matter what, I wasn't giving up.

"Awaken the Giant Within" turned out to be a terrific choice. The book flowed exceptionally well, and the psychology consumed me. I found myself reading for much lengthier stretches and more frequently. Before I knew it, in record time, I had completed the book. More importantly, I was able to extract three key principle concepts that helped me get control over my mental and emotional states.

The first principle I learned was the direct connection between habits, pleasure, and pain. Mainly, we associate practices with either pleasure or pain. Pavlov's dog is what came to mind, because similar to the dog salivating when it hears the bell, we immediately associate either comfort or discomfort with our habits. And, interestingly enough, frequently we have the incorrect association. For instance, let's say that you got introduced to new food such as ice cream, and you truly loved it and savored it. Yet, later that evening, you got sick from the flu unrelated to the food.

After that, every time you might see the ice cream, you may then associate it with a painful experience rather than the actual pleasurable experience and not want to eat it again. It was now an intriguing concept and one that resonated with me.

When I started my career in real estate, it only took me four phone calls to make $150,000. Yes, you heard right, ONLY 4 CALLS! And, back then, that was serious money. For instance, with that money, it was possible to buy three Ferraris. It, out and out, turned me into a "phone junky," where I would excitedly awake in the morning and be anxious to get to my office to "dial for dollars," as I called it.

It was an absolute adrenaline rush, and I was identical to Pavlov's salivating dog every day as I began to dial the phone. However, I had now been making my 100 calls per day routinely for years with no results, and there was no adrenaline for a fix. The conditioning had worn off, and it was more like running on a near-empty gas tank or even worse fumes, not knowing if there was a gas station in the near distance. Making those calls was outright distressing, yet I knew them to be necessary for me to succeed.

The second principal had to do with how thoughts, language, and patterns of behavior interweave with outcomes. An example being, if a person can understand how others accomplish specific things, then one may replicate that process and communicate it to others so they too may achieve it.

Further, language plays a part in the outcomes with positive word choices associated with positive results. This concept was developed in the 1970s by John Grinder, who was a linguist, and Richard Bandler, who was an information scientist and mathematician at the University of California. The concept floated in the ether for many years, flying below the radar. It took more than twenty-five years to become mainstream with the aid of the internet. Today it is commonly known by the acronym, NLP, short for Neuro-Linguistic Programming.

And the third principle of making your own rules and communicating them to the people around you for your happiness. It was a big one for me. I was worn down and tired from the constant negativity around me that included people sharing their pessimistic thoughts:

"Once you realize that you have already lost, you will have wished you had changed your mind sooner."

"Why don't you do something else already?"

"You know, it's only your time that you are wasting."

And on, and on, and on it went. I thought, "why don't these people keep their thoughts to themselves if they have nothing positive to say? However, we all know that many people can't help themselves. So, in my own best interest, I immediately implemented this strategy to find that the negative people stayed away. It was as if I had influenza, and they didn't want to catch anything from me. At first, I felt a bit guilty in the sense that I was pushing them away, but then I realized it was their choice, and it cleared the air and created neutral or positive space where I could get my work done without the dense clouds of doom looming overhead.

Before I knew it, I had finished the book. I now knew how to control my mental state and chose to take the position that failure is a matter of perception. And, to go a step further, failure is merely a point in time. Since I was still managing to scrape by, and I mean barely, I had not yet failed, and I would press on regardless until no longer possible.

I had been ridiculed, belittled, berated, and on and on and on, including dismissed by almost everyone around me. The most influential people in my life were at odds with me and reached the end of their rope. The challenge had escalated the situation to a level I could have never imagined, but I couldn't abandon what I knew to be true. And with that said, before I knew it, in what seemed like a blink of an eye, my entire life savings gone, and I had exhausted every idea I had discovered. What next?

CHAPTER 4

The Bittersweet Taste of Failure

> Many of life's failures are people who did not realize how close they were to success when they gave up.
>
> *THOMAS EDISON*

IT WAS A BEAUTIFUL Sunday afternoon as my wife and two small boys were napping inside our small but somewhat renovated two-bedroom single story cape cod looking home. I was at rock bottom! The lowest of the all-time mental lows and didn't want to tell my wife or anyone that it was game over. I didn't even know what to say or how to say it. It was elementary; we were just out of money, ideas, and options. The feeling was beyond nauseated. I could feel the crushing weight upon my chest once more. I knew what I had to do but, for some reason, couldn't bring myself to do it and spoil the weekend.

Instead, for no apparent reason, I opted for a smoke. Why? To this day, I still don't have a clue. I wasn't a smoker, but it seemed like the right thing to do at that moment. I mean, it was only one of the worst days of my entire life with hope nowhere in sight, so I guess what the f......?

I quietly slipped into our bedroom and past my wife as she napped in our bed. Straight into the walk-in closet, I went directly to the hook where she always hung her favorite purse. I'll never forget that purse; it was an Italian tan leather Il Bisonte backpack purse that she brought back from one her trips from Italy. It was worn, beyond its years with that weathered warm leather look that just felt like home. Inside, she kept a box of Marlboro Lights. I quickly flipped the top open and slid a single cigarette out of the pack, corralled the red lighter alongside, and ducked out to the front of the house to sit on the porch steps.

I sat down and the top porch step, I looked straight down and took a big sigh, I put the Marlboro in my mouth and reached to light it up with the red torch when out of the corner of my left eye I spotted a cheerfully young mother pushing a stroller towards our house. Without losing sight of her, I maintained my left eye locked on her, and without thinking twice, I casually lit the cigarette, looked up, smiled, and said, "Isn't it a beautiful day? And she replied, "yes, it certainly is! Hi I'm Kate, and this is my son Jack, we are new to the neighborhood."

I got up, and as I headed toward them, "Hey Kate and Jack, nice to meet you, I'm Keith." Jack was already three sheets to the wind. Fast asleep in the stroller with the blanket neatly tucked over the top and draped down, shielding him from the sun. I could tell Kate was absorbing the peace and serenity of the neighborhood and beautiful day by the smile that had graced her fair-skinned, freckled face.

We immediately began chatting, and I informed her about my wife and two boys. She then shared about the home they rented, and her husband, who was a writer. She was also very excited about the prospect of the kids becoming friends and being able to play together. She went on to tell me they had moved into the neighborhood from New York City, and they lived around the corner a few houses away. She had such good energy

I had forgotten about the big dilemma as we shared a handful of laughs over the differences between New York and Los Angeles. We then made tentative plans to get our families together and hangout, and within a matter of just a short few minutes, she was off. She and Jack disappeared around the corner. And, I thought to myself, "what a great moment!"

As I stood between the four-foot brick columns at the sidewalk that marked the entry path leading to the house, I could sense the energy flowing across my body. The sensation was similar to goosebumps, yet it was internal and traveled towards my heart. It was quite unlike anything I could remember. For no apparent reason I suddenly and miraculously felt so much better, an overwhelming feeling of hope enveloped me. I consciously decided to bury the remaining negative thoughts that had lingered from earlier in the day and deal with the inevitable tomorrow.

I then returned to the front steps of the house without the thought of smoking and took a seat. I sat there enjoying this newfound experience, and rather than question it or try to figure it out, I sat and allowed the moment to linger. It was as if time was standing still; I could feel the warmth of the day and the sunshine maintaining the comfort, and I knew everything would be okay.

The day soon progressed into evening, into the night, into the morning, and I soon found myself swigging my triple espresso and momentarily later standing in the dark outside Gold's gym as usual at 5:30 am.

I stayed in denial but managed to maintain a better than usual mood as I traded small talk with the usual suspects as I worked out. My sixty minutes passed, and I made my exit to get home to play with my boys and have breakfast with them and my wife before heading off to work. I took my shower, got dressed as if I had an Important meeting, had breakfast, said my goodbyes, and conveniently avoided my worst fear.

I arrived at the office and then looked around as if I was going to be saying goodbye and then picked up the phone and began making my usual 100 calls. They would take me until noon to complete, and hopefully, I could rustle the bushes in search of something golden. It was strange to me that even though I acknowledged the day before that it was game over, I continued calling. I laughed and thought to myself, not only are you living in denial but, your unbelievably stubborn or stupid.

A few hours passed and nothing as usual, so I took a walk to stretch my legs return and press on. It was great to get out into the open air and smell the fresh air and hear the trees whispering in the wind as the people bustled down the street on their breaks. I sat in the sun for what seemed like more than my share of time and then purposely headed back.

When I returned, there was a note on my desk from a gentleman. It had his name and number, and that was it, no message whatsoever. I turned around, walked out of my office, and approached the receptionist. "What did this guy want?" And as expected, she replied, "I have no idea, he wouldn't say." Of course, another sales call", I thought and to someone who has no money to buy anything, how ironic?

I went back into my office and sat down in my black leather executive chair that I had since I began working in real estate and reclined back, briefly elevating my legs onto my desk, as I debated whether or not to return the call. Of course, I was going to call him back and get it out of the way. After all, that was one of the first things I had learned from friends and associates that had more experience in business matters. Be efficient and address things without delay, otherwise, if you let them linger, no matter how small, things could get worse or an opportunity lost. It was hardly a disturbing moment. It was short and sweet as I picked up the phone to call without further delay.

I finessed the man's number along with the keypad and heard It ring, and it rang, and it rang, and it rang. "Of course, he's on another sales call, and I'll get his voicemail and have to get another call," I thought to myself. How annoying!

An unexpected, "Hello!" I was now off guard because I had been distracted. I fumbled and replied with a flustered wavering, "Ah, Hello, ah…… this is Keith Herman, and I am returning your call?" The gentleman replied, "Oh yes, Keith, thanks for reaching out to me." I was now perplexed and lost in my silence.

He replied, "Yes, I am interested in selling my apartment building. Your timing is perfect!"

YES!!! MUSIC TO MY EARS!

For a split second, I won the lottery. All I wanted to do was jump on my desk and dance like a fool. I did get many calls like this before, and they did result in me making lots of money. "This could be it?"

And then, "great, another lead," I thought!

Literally, in less than a microsecond, the wind left my sails, as if stolen by an invisible thief, and it was back to the negative state of the general climate around me. And then, all the self-doubting questions began to follow in my head:

> "I can only imagine how ridiculous his price is?"

> "Even if the price is reasonable, how will I get the deposit to secure the contract?"

> "Even if the price is reasonable and I get the deposit, who will be the buyer?"

> And, on and on and on

Before I allowed my mind to take me down the road to failure, I recovered, and my years of conditioning took over. I began asking him my standard questions about the property.
Like:

> How long have you owned it?
> What is the gross income?
> What is the current occupancy?
> What is the mix of units? And, so on....
> And then, my final question as always,
> "So, why sell now?"

CHAPTER 5

Eureka

EUREKA!!!

What followed next was music to my ears, and now I did have reason to dance on the desk. The seller explained to me that the property had been in his family for generations, and he and his sister recently inherited the property. Neither one of them wanted to take care of it anymore. Although they didn't need to sell it, and it meant a great deal to them, they felt it was time to let it go from the family and move on.

The trumpets sounded, and I was now genuinely excited! I had a motivated Seller, the price they were asking was more than reasonable, and they were emotionally attached to the property. It was like a slot machine in Las Vegas pulling up three of a kind on each wheel for the big payout. It was a huge windfall!

From experience, I knew that the ownership transition could be very advantageous if done cooperatively and cordially. In other words, very often, sellers in such situations will be very accommodating to get the property sold to the right buyer.

It was now time for me to work my magic. When the conversation was over, he agreed to allow me to buy the property with very little down payment, with them providing the financing for the balance of the sale. In other words, they made me a loan for what amounted to 90% of the sale price. They also gave me an allowance for some repairs and to renovate some units to make them rent-ready, which further reduced the down payment requirement.

All tolled, I was able to reach an agreement where I only needed to put up less than 5% of the purchase price to buy the property. It was genuinely incredible considering that buildings in this location were so desirable that people were willing to pay considerably more than what I was paying and, from time to time, pay "ALL CASH."

WOW, WHAT A DEAL!!!

IN A MATTER OF AN HOUR, I WAS NOW FLYING HIGH!

Oh, "But I have no money to buy this property or even dinner for my family, who will be hungry in a matter of a few hours."

"Jesus, I'm so damn close! If I can only bridge this gap, I'll be way back in business," I thought. "What do I focus on now? Food for dinner or this property?" I am now in a quandary between excitement and nervousness. I dash out of the office for another brisk walk. This time I couldn't see a thing; it was strictly business with no time to wander off. I did the six blocks in no time flat, and the jitters were gone.

In record time! I was back at the office and ready to prepare the Purchase and Sale Agreement. It was a four-page Agreement on legal size paper with a light blue background. It was a standard Agreement drafted by the California Real Estate Association and approved by the California Department of Real Estate. It was perfect because it was very official looking and very neutral to the parties. The result was that people would sign them all the time without a lawyer because they seemed so fair on their face.

It was a triplicate document, which meant that there were copies attached with carbon paper in between the pages to make copies instantly. This way, once everyone signed the Agreement, they were able to tear off a copy for their records, and the original went to the escrow company that handled the transaction to its conclusion.

It had about 30 clauses in tiny black font, a few fill-in-the-blank sections to cover things like the names of the Buyer and Seller, and the address and parcel number of the property. There were also a few bold sections in scary prominent bold capital print for the worst-case scenario sections such as "Termination" and "Liquidated Damages." It is where you could lose your deposit, so the Department of Real Estate wanted to make sure everyone was paying close attention in case of a dispute. And, then finally, the most critical section…. "**Other Terms & Conditions**."

For me, this is where things got very interesting. In my eyes, the "Other Terms & Conditions" section is what separated the professionals from the amateurs. When real estate agents, or the boys, were crafting this section, they generally included just a few extra brief sentences to address minor changes to the Agreement. After all, that is considered the norm; less is more meaning there would be fewer terms to possibly dispute. However, for the men, this was the heart of the Agreement. It was the perfect opportunity to maximize the Agreement to accommodate all sorts of situations. And, it was an opportunity for me to put my creativity and ditched legal education to work.

I began completing it, wholly and thoroughly, checking every entry at least twice before proceeding. Back then, the options for correcting typewriters were limited, so slow and careful was not just the rule but a necessity. Otherwise, it could have meant having to start all over again. Or, one error or omission could have cost the entire deposit posted for the transaction.

Finally, I reached the "Other Terms & Conditions," and I pulled my signature move! I typed in …… SEE ATTACHED ADDENDUM.

It was comical to me. Without exception, I would chuckle each time I would get to it. Because I knew that even though this was the most crucial section, most of the time, by the time the Seller would get to read it, they were mentally spent and just wanted to get the transaction over with and would sign all the pages out of sheer exhaustion.

I began to sculpt my future as I filled out the Addendum. I was visualizing money in my now empty bank account, no mounds of debt, no debt collectors continually calling, nobody pestering me about how crazy I am and a much-needed vacation. The sound of the roaring fork river in Colorado filled my head, the sensation of warm water and a fly-fishing rod in my hand overcame me. I was drifting off quickly, and it was tempting to go with the moment, but I couldn't afford to waste another minute, I had to get dinner on the table.

I snapped out of it and focused on the Addendum staring at me from behind the typewriter ball. I noticed I was now sweating; I pushed on pecking away one finger at a time in the hopes of finishing speedily. I made sure to preserve my deposit, get credits for improvements, and get the property for as little cash as possible. I finished up with the final period and checked everything with precision. I was brimming with pride; I had not made a single error or omitted a single critical point.

Time was of the essence. I glimpsed at the clock as I plucked the Addendum from the "money machine," as I called it. I seized all of the documents and slipped them smoothly into a brand new dull legal-sized manila folder to make things look more official. From there, I opened my briefcase, not much more than a casual bag not to intimidate, and made certain my two lucky pens were inside and full of ink. I placed the folder inside and zipped it shut.

And now, with a spring in my step, I made a break for the car to drive across town. It was time to secure the man's signature. I didn't even ponder what was waiting for me or what might happen. All I knew was I was confident the this was going to happen and timely.

I allowed the excitement to suppress my negative thoughts. It was a constant battle between the two, but I was going to be damned if I let the negative win, so I concentrated on my blaring favorite tunes. I sang along aloud in the LA traffic, at times, feeling self-conscious and even moronic at times, but with the help of something greater than myself, I arrived in perfect spirits.

I pulled into the driveway of the man's home, came to a stop, and almost puked. The pressure was paralyzing, "I mean, even if he signs the papers, I have no money to buy the property, and I've got more immediate problems." The internal dialogue was unquestionably crushing me.

I fell back into the warm contoured clothed seat of the car, gently sealed my eyes shut, and gave out a few sizable exhales until nothing was left. I advanced with a slow and methodical breath until nausea passed. I waited until my mind went bright and then gradually opened my eyes. "LET'S DO THIS!"

I hurriedly opened the car door and exited only to find myself standing on the gentlemen's well-manicured lawn. "Oh, crap!" I blurted. I was ridiculously paranoid and concerned that I might offend the man, and he might not sign the papers, so in an instant, I twirled onto the path leading to the entry. I zipped along soon to be staring at the doorbell. I rang it with purpose, and within a few seconds, the door flung open. From the shadowy darkness, I faintly heard a soft voice utter, "Hi Keith, come in."

I ignored my initial impression of despair and followed my gut through the door. I emerged the temporary barrier of doom to an Asian oasis with colorful rugs and tapestries and furniture sparsely occupying the space. There were a handful of large pots strategically placed throughout, all of which sat upon exquisitely carved pedestals and contained an array of artfully placed plants.

There were also a few mini bamboo plants and mini bonsai trees scattered around, and next to the dining table, my eyes glommed onto a Pachira Aquatica. Also known as a Guiana Chestnut, Saba Nut, or "Money Tree." The sandalwood incense fragrance in the air caught my nose and reminded me of home. I thought to myself, "Things could not be more perfect!"

He coaxed me over to the dining room table, where we settled to discuss the transaction. However, suddenly I was in no rush. I felt so comfortable; it was as if time had stopped. He asked me about myself, and instead of diving into the obvious right off the bat, I lead with complimenting him on his taste and showed off my limited knowledge of Asian design and furnishings, which he much appreciated.

He eventually transitioned over to the property and shared its history and its place within their family. I listened attentively to the anecdotes he shared and waited until he finally purged himself of its presence. And then, with impeccable timing, I explained to him how I needed their help to get the property spruced up to be able to get them paid in full.

He truly appreciated the time and consideration I had put into carefully contemplating their needs and desires. Unlike many other folks I had dealt with over the years, that inherited property and just wanted to get rid of it to get the money, this was more like letting a child go off into the world. Without hesitation, he suggested we review the paperwork quickly, and without even offering, he asked for my pen and signed each page without vacillation.

"And now you'll have to forgive me. I have another commitment," the man said. He cautiously stood up, escorted me to the door, and asked that I keep him informed on how to proceed and what if anything else I would need. Things could not have gone any smoother, mission accomplished! But it wasn't quite time to start dancing.

CHAPTER 6

Where's Dinner

HOPPED INTO THE car and exited as quickly as possible without appearing to be in a rush. What a relief! But what now? Where shall I head? I'm due for dinner shortly, and what do I have? I have a contract to purchase a property, perhaps food for thought but indeed not dinner.

I drove a handful of blocks and then veered into a no-name gas station. I spotted a space just off to the side where I could gather my thoughts. With exhaustion, I could taste victory, but the adrenaline was frankly fading fast like the fumes of an empty tequila shot. "Just don't panic, and you'll be fine," said a voice in my head. At that moment, I felt throughout my body; it was true.

I went back to my faithful breathing exercise and peacefully peered open my eyes. Smack in my face was the clock as if it had grown quadruple in size, with time expiring. "This isn't helping," I thought. "I gotta move NOW!" I popped open the door and started to jog down the sidewalk. I could smell the trees in bloom and then the smell of dinner as I passed an apartment building with a bar-b-que smoking away. "This is crazy," I thought, but what else to do?

I sat down on what looked like the patchy burnt grass of some stranger's front lawn and thought, why am I avoiding? And as quickly as I posed, the question to the answer came. It was me! I was running from failure! I was afraid I was going to fail. How bizarre, I thought, since I was doing everything to succeed.

I was remembering, like as if it was yesterday sitting crossed legged on that half grass, half dirt front lawn saying adamantly aloud, "I will not fail!" I was mad I'm talking downright pissed off with myself as I had never been before! I wanted to go fist to fist with myself! How, could I? I got this far, and I had what it took to get the rest of the way. I wasn't quitting.

I instinctively let go of the anger like releasing a weight belt that held me submerged underwater as my air was expiring. I unclipped the belt and immediately felt free to move, free to breathe, free to think, free to finish what I started. And with that, I stood up and walked back to the car.

As I plodded back to the car and studied the sidewalk to avoid the cracks, I agreed with myself not to even revisit or address the past or consider the potential adverse outcomes.

It was a long walk, and it was liberating, it was cathartic, refreshing, perfect, exactly what I needed. And, I still had about an hour to get the deal put together.

I found my car, where I left it and headed off back to my office. Along the drive, Steven Fogel's book came to mind and how he explained assessing your resources. I then began compiling a mental list of all the people that could perhaps help me put the money together. It wasn't very long and wasn't exactly ideal since the thought of approaching anyone one of those people filled me with trepidation. Nevertheless, I was planning to call each and everyone one of them.

As I neared the end of the list, I was becoming more and more apprehensive. It just wasn't sitting well with me. I needed something different in the mix, but what? Who was I missing? I wasn't getting what I wanted. I began reflecting on anyone that I recently met that even took an interest in me either personally or professionally.

And then it hit me! A transient memory of someone I was relatively recently introduced to that understood finances very well. We had met briefly through an acquaintance perhaps two or three times max but never really had the opportunity to get to know each other. "Seriously?" I thought to myself, "you don't even really know the person. You truly are crazy." However, desperate times call for extreme measures.

I instantly changed course on a dime, and, ahead of everyone I was going to call on the list, I decided on a gut feeling to visit them on the fly. No appointment, no call first, show up cold. "Hardly, good use of time, everything considered. Sheer stupidity, insanity or brilliance at its finest", I thought. I spent the remainder of the drive vacillating between sheer stupidity and sheer insanity. "I mean, what the hell is up with me?" but I needed to know.

I arrived at their office and low and behold found a parking space right in front. How lucky and without delay slid the car cleanly back into the parking space and threw the car into park. At this point, the adrenaline was running high, and all fear had left the body. Quite impressive, yet quite scary. I mean, who in their right mind does this kind of thing of stuff? The thoughts just kept coming. I got out and fed the meter, and headed into the building straight for their office.

I strolled through the door with a temperate and genuine smile on my face, opening with a big, "Hey, how are you?" Hardly surprised to see me, as if to see unannounced visitors often. The retort was a breezy, "Hey, nice to see you. I'm good, come on in and have a seat." I inserted myself into the nearest chair, and then what proceeded resembled more of a heart to heart between old friends than anything else. Before I knew it, I was popping the question for a temporary loan, and without missing a beat earned a resounding, YES!

I knew it! I knew it! I knew it! And there you have it! Not only did I leave with the tens of thousands of dollars needed to complete the purchase of the property, but I had also just made a deal, and they gave me the money in cash.

Yes, cash! A big brown bag full of bills! I had not seen so much cash at one time since I was a little kid when I would go collecting money with my dad from the donut shops in the subways of New York City. We would go from shop to shop accumulating cash, and then about every five stops would go upstairs to meet my grandfather, who would later deposit the money.

The big difference this time around was the cash was for me, and the bills were much more substantial. It was like I had just robbed a bank and now had to get away without anyone noticing me. To a certain extent, I was terrified I might get held up and be back at square one and yet at the same time ecstatic that my dream was coming true. I now had the cash I needed to get the deal done and put dinner on the table and celebrate with my unbelievably supportive wife and two young boys. Life was great. I was once again riding high and hooked on the impossible!

Having just solved one of the biggest challenges of my life, I now had to focus on getting enough cash to live, until I could get the property turned around and sold. I knew this was no easy task, but I couldn't imagine it being anywhere near as stressful as what I had just pulled off. With that in mind, I began going down my list. Before long, I finished with rejection after rejection.

"To hell with the list!", I thought. It was back to Fogel's way of thinking. I knew there had to be a way to solve the dilemma. Once again, it would require a change in my perspective, my thinking, or both. So, I went back to the basics. I looked at what I had to work with, which included the property I just purchased.

I commenced with combing over the financials to see if it was possible to squeeze some money out it. The building made no money and needed money to fix it up. Hardly a reason to believe it was possible to squeeze any money out, but I took a close look at the operations and figured out a way to use the rents and float expenses in such a manner that I could squeeze out somewhere between 60-90 days of living capital. I carefully revisited the idea a few times and confirmed that it was possible.

I couldn't leave anything to chance, so I carefully planned out the whole scenario. I pushed and pushed and pushed to get the property turned around even faster to shave down the time in my favor. Before I knew it, I had renovated the building and had it up for sale. Within a few weeks, after that, I was under contract with a non-refundable deposit released to me. And, it was just the amount of money I needed to carry me to the closing date where I would then receive a big chunk of cash. Enough cash to pay-off all my debts and have money to take me for a good stretch.

In my eyes, I had just come off an incredible journey— one where I narrowly dodged a fatal bullet. I was a fortunate man to emerge an ordeal I wouldn't wish upon anyone. A situation that lasted roughly five years and one that I would never forget! One that showed me who I was and what I could endure. It taught me about the human condition, both physical and mental. It taught me about the challenges we face each day and how we handle them. I was a lucky man and didn't want to do it twice. "Perhaps I should reflect and better understand what just happened before rushing off on the next adventure? Who knows how long the next one will be or what it will entail? And so, I did!

As I reflected on the harrowing journey, I somehow miraculously survived, I came to the following realizations:

1. "Point of View" makes all the difference in the world, and the more we have and the more open we are to each one of them, the higher the possibility we may succeed.

Why was this important? My experience showed me that it is easier to fail when you have fewer options available. In other words, it is essential to have as many options as possible to help you achieve success. After all, in most cases, we are talking about making your desires, goals, and dreams and not something insignificant such as what meal you would ideally like to have for dinner. My observations led me to believe that people generally try something, fail, try again, fail and then quickly accept failure as their reality and move on feeling defeated, less than satisfied, unworthy, and in many cases, depressed. There is no reason that more people can't achieve their desires, goals, dreams, and happiness; they need more options along the way to help them.

2. "Failure" is related to your point of view in the sense that failure is not necessarily perceived to be the same by everyone, meaning people's points of view vary, and it is only a moment in time defined by whoever chooses to call it a failure.

Why was this important? My experience showed me that in many other people's eyes, they were quick to judge me as a failure based upon their point of view and repeated negative and often demeaning comments.

However, I did not share their point of view. From my point of view, I wasn't a failure at all. It was a challenge in my pursuit of what I truly wanted. We can go back and forth and say, "from one particular point you were failing and therefore considered a failure." However, the converse may also be true. "Perhaps that looked to be the case, but because I ultimately prevailed, I was never a failure!" The point here is that the perception of failure can make all the difference in the world! It is the difference between quitting and succeeding and can be decided in an instant if chosen.

Based on my life experience, I have always been able to succeed in achieving the things that truly mattered to me. I never viewed the challenges along the way as failures merely hurdles. In fairness, sometimes I went over them, sometimes through them and sometimes around them, but the important thing was that I always finished the race. Somethings took more effort than others, but ultimately it came down to how bad I wanted them. It is these two fundamental points, "Point of View" and "Failure," I believe to be at the core of success.

CHAPTER 7

The Greatest Hurdle

Success – favorable or desired outcome.
Failure – lack of success.

BY MERIAM-WEBSTER

Success and Failure are contrary to each other!

TO BEST UNDERSTAND SUCCESS, it is imperative to understand its counterpart, FAILURE! As I've repeatedly stated, I'm a supreme fan of perspective or point of view because I firmly believe it to be a substantive component to success and failure. In the previous chapter, you may recall that I never referred to any part of my journey as a "Failure." In my particular case, I did achieve the favorable or desired outcome I sought. Therefore, according to Merriam-Webster, I did achieve success.

> I Can Accept Failure, Everyone Fails at Something. But I Can't Accept Not Trying.
>
> MICHAEL JORDAN

Michael Jordan makes the keen observation that not "Trying" can lead to "Failure." And, we all know that Michael Jordan did try. He self-admittedly was a mediocre basketball player growing up, but by "Trying," his best became arguably the best basketball player in the history of basketball.

So, why exactly do we fail? And why is it so important to know the answer? To answer these questions, it is helpful to exam the most often mentioned excuses for failure. These excuses include a lack of self-esteem, persistence, conviction, discipline, rationalizing, fatalistic attitude, and horrible past mistakes.

Poor self-esteem is a lack of confidence in ones' abilities. It may be for a variety of reasons, such as lack of courage, self-respect, or self-worth. It keeps people preoccupied with their identity, more specifically finding who they are rather than creating their character. Being focused on realizing yourself to a large extent takes your attention off the present and thereby limits your scope of opportunities, which reduces possibilities and potential successful outcomes. Similarly, lacking self-worth creates doubt and distraction, which also reduces focus and limits outcomes and the likelihood of succeeding.

Often claimed for giving up is a lack of persistence. It is usually for no apparent or valid reason, such as a lack of knowledge. Lack of conviction may also appear as someone taking the middle road or merely looking to conform with others. As soon the going gets tough or the others bail, so do they. Lack of discipline is where people don't have the self-control to make sacrifices and resist temptations. They are often compulsive in their decisions and get derailed easily regardless of the resources at hand. Rationalization is also frequently cited for those that have a litany of excuses not to proceed. Fatalistic attitude is where people possess the misbelief that success all comes down to luck, and since chance doesn't appear to be on their side this time around, there is no point in continuing. And, terrible past mistakes that only lead to repeating them with the same unhappy ending.

At face value, these do not offer us real reasons for failure. They are merely excuses. Therefore, to honestly know why we fail, we must look beyond the explanations to the root cause. A deeper dive into the reasons mentioned and Michael Jordan's quote, all point to a common thread, and it is "mental states" or "state of mind."

I'm sure you have experienced being in a bad mood for one reason or another. An example is your significant other intentionally threw away your favorite article of clothing and then attempted to convince you is in your best interest. After all, it made you look considerably less appealing and then dusted the matter off as if the whole thing were no big deal. How receptive would you be to listening to what your significant other had to say after that? Probably not very! Or let's say, your boss promoted someone less qualified than you just because they liked them and tried to convince you they were best for the job. How would you feel, and how likely would you be to listen to your boss, moving forward? Probably, not very likely! The point is, we all get to a point where we decided that the negativity is too much, and we block what is incoming. Even if the inbound is positive and for our benefit.

Now, imagine that you could routinely control your mental state entirely and not get disrupted by these types of situations. You would then have the opportunity to allow positive things to come through and potentially take advantage of them. Going back to the first example, what if you looked fifty pounds heavier in your favorite article of clothing, and it would genuinely bother you. If you were open to seeing the situation objectively, you most likely would be okay with saying goodbye to the article of clothing. Said another way, when we are in a positive state of mind, we are more open to receiving possibilities that offer us more potential outcomes and a higher likelihood of success. It also eliminates the need for excuses. Categorically, "mental state" or "state of mind" is the number one reason for failure and, therefore, *"The Greatest Hurdle"* to Success!!!"

Now that we have answered the first question, "why do we fail?" the answer to the second question becomes more germane. It is essential to know why we fail so that we can have a solution to help avoid failure. To clear *"The Greatest Hurdle,"* it's crucial to understand better what is necessary to do so.

"Awareness" is the knowledge or perception of a situation and is top of the list. Going back to the E-Myth and the top-down approach, imagine if we started to construct a very tall building with no plans whatsoever. Imagine what will happen if the building does not have a well-established foundation supporting it, the building will ultimately collapse under its weight. With just a single flaw in the foundation, the building would collapse. It is why we have architects carefully draw plans and even for simple single-story structures.

Similarly, with Awareness, if one is only aware of what they see on the ground floor, they cannot see what is going on above them, which may impede their progress or ability to solve a problem. An example would be attempting to build a tall structure only to find that a freeway exists above you. Similarly, in the words of Albert Einstein, a higher state of consciousness (awareness) is necessary to solve problems at the level of consciousness (awareness) at which they arise. In other words, the more you are aware, the more you can see and the more possibilities that exist, which offers more potential outcomes and a higher probability for a successful outcome.

Our Desire is a strong feeling to want to have something or something happen, is a mental state, and by itself is harmless. Being aware of why you have the desire, provides a distinct advantage. Because Desire looks to motivation to get the job done, and the two go hand in hand, meaning the more significant the Desire, the more significant the motivation that can be applied. Therefore, if you know the reason why you desire something, you can then consciously use the proper amount of motivation to achieve what you want.

Motivation is the reason one has for acting or behaving in a particular manner. It inspires us to achieve the goal we seek and, therefore, a critical factor in outcomes. Hence, it is essential to be aware of our motivation before commencing achieving an outcome. There are two types of motivation internal motivation & external motivation, knowing the difference delivers a key advantage because one provides much better results.

External motivation is when someone acts a certain way for external reasons such as for money or coercion. If the external motivation is insufficient, such as too little money, then the desired result may likely not occur. However, internal motivation is when a person does something for their own sake because of their inner beliefs without any external reward. In these situations, the motivation is much more compelling and more likely to produce the desired results.

Consider someone who offers you five dollars to jump off a twenty-foot bridge into the deep water below. The external motivation of five dollars may not be enough for you to take the plunge. However, if someone put a gun to your head and you believed they would pull the trigger, that internal belief of possible death would most likely provide enough motivation for you to jump off the bridge into the water below quickly.

Belief is an acceptance that something is real or it exists. Being aware of whether or not something exists is also a distinct advantage. If you believe in something that does not exist, then you cannot succeed in obtaining it. An example, you think you can purchase a brand-new car from a car dealer at the 7/11 down the street. No matter how strong your belief, you won't be able to buy the vehicle if no car dealer exists at the 7/11.

Also, the likelihood of achieving something you do not believe exists even if it does is less because you possess less conviction and motivation. An example, you don't think you can get a free pizza on National Pizza day from Domino's Pizza. Even though they are giving away pizza, it is your belief there is no such place as Domino's Pizza. Therefore, you have no conviction or motivation even to attempt to get the pizza.

Now, suppose you think you can get the free pizza from Dominos on National pizza. In this case, the belief is enough to motivate you to take the drive, which gives you the advantage to reap the reward. Your Beliefs are critical because they determine whether or not you will take action. That, in turn, directly impacts your chances of success.

Planning, deciding on, or arranging in advance is also a factor for success. Consider making a road trip cross country with your best friends. You all pile into the car and head out. You have no specific destination, route, or knowledge of where to stop along the way for essentials such as fuel, lodging, or even food. What is the likelihood you will reach the coast without getting lost, running out of gas, or encountering a whole host of other challenges?

On the contrary, you not only plan the trip and make sure you head in the correct direction, but you also plan for stops along the way to address potential needs along the way. Without question, a proper and well-thought-out plan increases the likelihood of success.

Action or the process of doing something to achieve an aim is paramount to success. It is the action that moves you toward your goal. Taking Action commensurate with your Desire and Motivation increases the likelihood of success.

Imagine you Desire a vacation, a much-needed vacation! You are now Motivated to ask for your time off because you have the Belief you have the time coming. You Plan to ask your boss tomorrow for the time off. You're now brimming with excitement thinking of lying on that warm terry clothed sheathed chaise lounge under the straw umbrella on the white sand beach as you watch the waves slosh on shore with a margarita in your hand while you're listening to your favorite tune.

You wake in the morning after barely sleeping from excitement and take action by going into work to ask for the time off. You haul into the parking lot; slide into the first space you see. You throw the car into park as you slip out of your seat belt and unhinge the door. You hurry into the build, through the lobby, and up the elevator. Past the receptionist, you go, "Hey Laura, you look wonderful today!" and straight to the boss's office to hear him bellow, "don't even think of asking me for time off when we are in the middle of this fiasco!" to another colleague.

You perilously jam on the brakes and fall just shy of his door. The Aware person you are realizes that perhaps Action is not the Plan at the moment. You pull yourself together and retreat to your office to give him space and time to cool off. You regroup and decide to postpone the conversation for tomorrow to increase your likelihood of succeeding. And, this is how we all maneuver towards success!

So far, we have looked at Awareness, Desire, Motivation, Belief, Planning, Action, and now it's time to explore two other elements, Values, and Destiny. First, Values or a person's principals or standards are things we believe deep down and are essential in the way we live your life and work. They also have a direct bearing on your Motivation.

If our Values are not in alignment with our Beliefs, then we will lack the Motivation to take Action and thereby diminish our chances for success. Therefore, it is imperative to be aware that these are aligned to maximize the odds of success; very often, they are not.

Case in point, perhaps you value friendships more than money and believe deep down that you must honor this belief or there will be repercussions on some level. You then launch a bootstrapping healthy potato chip company with your best friend JJ that you've known since kindergarten and played with every day after school. You would frequent each other homes and enjoy eating potato chips together and spending considerable time with each other's families.

You then get approached by an acquaintance that is impressed with your business savvy and offers you big bucks for virtually the same business you are in with JJ and only asks for ten (10%) percent ownership, far less than JJS's fifty (50%). You can't help yourself, and you accept the offer leaving JJ devasted, and both your families and friends mad at you. You tell yourself they will all get over it, and you press on. Everyone remains upset with you, and the challenges begin with no one to talk to, not even your bankrolling buddy, because he knows nothing about the business.

With your network and your support system, now gone, it becomes much more mentally challenging to maintain the Motivation and to keep a clear mind for the right decisions. With fewer people to help with the challenges, the odds of succeeding then become less than had you stayed with JJ because at least with JJ, you would have had someone to share the burden of the challenges and both of your resources and support systems available. Having your Values and Beliefs aligned to make things much smoother because they eliminate inner conflict and are the "grease for peace" to get you to success.

And finally, Destiny or the hidden power believed to control what will happen in the future is an essential factor in achieving success. Destiny is vital because it, too, speaks to your deep-rooted beliefs. If you believe it is your Destiny, then similarly to Values, you will follow your Destiny, which thereby increases the likelihood of successfully achieving it. Again, we are talking about alignment and "greasing the wheels" to achieve success.

Understanding these elements and how they affect success makes it easier to see how people accomplish what seems to be impossible. I like to use Michael Jordan as an example because he did achieve what most people thought to be impossible, and his backstory known, making it pretty clear how he was able to achieve such incredible success.

For Michael, the road to success was filled with countless challenges to get to become a professional athlete. He not only didn't make his high school basketball team at Laney High School in Wilmington, North Carolina his sophomore year but he admitted:

> "I've missed more than 9,000 shots in my career. I've lost almost 300 games. Twenty-six times, I've been trusted to take the game-winning shot and missed. I've failed over and over and over again in my life. And that is why I succeed."

His statement displays on its face that his determination, which is reflective of mental states, including self-esteem, persistence, conviction, discipline, and positive attitude, got him the positive results. He also chose not to rationalize his shortcomings instead of learning from his mistakes. This winning combination eliminated the common excuses for failure we often hear and sent him in the direction of success. It also propelled him to the uber-successful athlete he became. So, what exactly was going on at the mental level? How was he able to maintain the mental states needed to avoid failure?

CHAPTER 8

The Perfect View

THE ANSWER IS "CONSCIOUSNESS." Consciousness is the state of being awake and knowing of one's surroundings or a situation or fact. It's also referred to as awareness. If you have more knowledge and or perception, you have a broader view. That more comprehensive view includes more vantage points or points of view (POV). As I mentioned, more viewpoints equal more possibilities and more opportunities to achieve success.

Everyone's journey begins with Consciousness. Michael's case is no different. Michael had the thought or idea to play basketball on his high school team, and that led to his Desire or feeling of actually wanting to play on the basketball team.

Next, from his Desire, his Motivation was born. In his particular case, we know that, according to Michael's father, he had always been an overly competitive child. He had a distinct deep-down burning Desire for as long as he could remember that he wanted to fulfill. Perhaps he was inspired by a particular basketball player he idolized and wanted to follow in his footsteps. Or maybe he believed in being the best at everything he enjoyed to derive maximum pleasure. These are both examples of internal Motivation, and Michael most certainly had it.

So, the question became whether or not the Belief existed that the outcome would happen. We know Michael had the Belief because he took the next step that involved preparing for the tryout. It may have been some minimal practice or perhaps long practice sessions. Regardless of what that Plan entailed, he was willing to show up and try out, which he did. Unfortunately, his Belief, when tested, proved his Action to be insufficient, and he failed to make the team.

Having gone through this process, we can see that somewhere something went awry. Somewhere, there was a breakdown in the process because the result was failing to make the team. Looking back and examining every step, we can better understand where exactly the process broke down. And, once we can identify precisely where the process broke down, we are then able to ask why and further investigate how to improve upon the method that previously failed.

We know from Michael's history and Action that he was very much aware or Conscious, and he had the Desire and Motivation along with the Belief he could make the team. He also had a Plan and took Action. So, where was the breakdown?

Perhaps looking at the situation in reverse or from the top down, as described in the E-Myth, will bring clarity? We know that the Action was unsatisfactory because he didn't make the team. It would then lead us to question the validity of his Plan. Again, based upon the outcome, the Plan didn't seem to work either. So, we must then examine his Belief, and it's safe to say that he had the Belief he had a shot at making the team because he took Action and did try out.

However, he may not have had a full-hearted Belief that he would make the team, and that would make a difference. Hence, this may have been a sticking point. With Belief in question, we would then look to his Motivation. And, we know it was internal, but did it contribute to the failure? Based on what we know, it's possible, but the answer is probably not.

Nevertheless, it's then worth looking to his Desire, and he certainly had the desire to continue the process, so the question becomes, was it sufficient enough to possess the Motivation. It appears the answer is yes. His father made clear that Michael was an overly competitive child, which is indicative of strong Desire. In conclusion, as we can see from the analysis, there was more than one fault in Michael's process, and that is most likely why he did not prevail in making the team.

It begs the prodigious question, what exactly were the corrections he made that were the impetus for him eventually making the team and rocketing to superstardom? I suppose one could easily say that he naturally decided to focus and call it a day. However, we all know you don't just go onto superstardom by merely focusing your attention. How many times have you placed your focus on something and got the result you wanted, let alone the kind that got you worldwide recognition?

Must it have been something compelling? And it was! He did not remain Conscious enough to maintain the perfect mental states in "ALIGNMENT." Yes, Alignment! Doing so, greased the wheels to Success! Complete, Alignment requires not only Consciousness but the ability to juxtapose Consciousness with Desire, Motivation, Belief, Planning, Action, Values & Destiny. We are talking about a level of Consciousness that is a skill, and it grants you the capability to scrutinize each of these elements from various points of view to identify faults so you may develop an optimal solution.

> "My attitude is if you push me towards something that you think is a weakness, then I will turn that perceived weakness into a strength."
>
> MICHAEL JORDAN

Michael's Consciousness was consistently providing mental views and clues as he observed other's actions and thoughts as well as his own. He would probe them carefully, reach conclusions, and then act to produce the best result. By repeating this process, he would tweak his thoughts to keep his mental states aligned and improve his performance. Michael possessed the Desire, Motivation, and Belief that his Destiny was to be a great athlete and knew it would require hard work. He adjusted his Values, Plan, and Action through points of view to Align with his Desire, Motivation, and Belief to realize his Destiny. It was no case of luck! It was sheer brilliance executed to perfection!

And now that we understand by way of example how to achieve SUCCESS, I'll show you how one entrepreneur achieved success to the tune of $12 Million from a non-descript, unassuming shoebox.

CHAPTER 9

Meet My Boyfriend

2010, THE YEAR OF The Haiti Earthquake, BP Oil Spill, WikiLeaks, Times Square Bomber, Toy Story 3, Black Swan, The Social Network, Eat Pray Love, Tick Tok, Need You Now, Hey, Soul Sister. California Girls, Super Bowl Saints, NBA Lakers, world Series Giants, iPad, Kickstarter, Square, Google's Driverless Car, Electric-Car Charging Stations, 3-D Bioprinter and Lab-Grown Lungs. There was plenty of sorrow, action, excitement, disruption, joy, innovation, and wonder in the air. It was chaotic, despairing, novel, inspiring, worrying, hopeful, and a time for giving.

The piercing alarm erupted from my phone, and I sprung to attention. For a moment, I sat upright as if to stretch and then relaxed back into my comfortable leather-wrapped executive chair from behind my computer monitor that sat upon my lengthy absolute black granite desk. I had lost track of time as usual and now gazed out my expansive office window in Beverly Hills, admiring the mountains and downtown view. It was another beautiful day in Southern California, but I knew it was time for me to go. I needed to conveniently cruise down the street to an event at the Beverly Hilton Hotel to hear aspiring entrepreneurs pitch their promising technology endeavors.

I made way to the Hotel and pulled up to the valet. "Hey, where's the tech event," I uttered. "Through the glass doors and then veer off to the right once you are in the lobby," the valet replied. I pursued the path and found the tall narrow doors soon visible. A small podium with a placard and the event details were immediately in front of the entry. The crisp crème statuesque doors sat half open with a loud rumble of anxious folks chatting away.

The event was about to get underway, with the vanilla room filled with people in rows of conference hall chairs that sat in parallel rows lined from the rear straight to the front of the room that hosted the minimalist stage. I scanned the room for a place to sit and promptly squeezed passed a few dozen smartly dressed attendees and claimed the seat.

The MC took the stage and calmed the audience to get the event moving. First up was a prominent former executive from IBM to pitch a new technology startup he had proudly joined. I listened attentively to realize soon it was going nowhere fast, a real dud. There were countless issues with the concept and execution problems, and we promptly knew he was merely a figurehead. He finished with a big fat grin and was soon eviscerated by the fans as he toiled with every question. It was painful to watch!

I browsed the program and soon lost faith in the prospects. I rose and smoothly made my way past the smartly dressed attendees that had become crotchety and ducked out of the room straight to the lobby. There was a small group of people that had coalesced near the seating area adjacent to the bar and were graciously exchanging their business cards. "I made the trip, so why waste it," I thought.

There were investors, entrepreneurs, developers, service providers, and who knows who else. Into my upper jacket pocket, I reached where I always had kept a stash of business cards. "Excuse me while I whip this out," I said to break the old crowd. One of my favorite movie lines from "Blazing Saddles," usually well-received while networking back in the day. I got a few chuckles as expected and then worked my magic.

Exchanging cards was the name of the game, and I did it well. I grabbed them quickly, along with the owner's quick teaser. Now armed, my sites peered on the exit with plans to rebound to the office. The cards would soon lie on my desk for a cool twenty-four hours before I would reach out to anyone of interest.

I blazed back to my saddle to get another glimpse of the view before settling in to review more offering memorandums and pitch decks before heading home to the kids for dinner. It was my typical day, and the majority of it filled with exciting opportunities. It was an adventure as I habitually was combing through materials left and right and networking with friends, acquaintances, and a cast of characters for a needle in a haystack to grab my attention and potentially my time and money.

I had learned a boatload since my first tech investment back in 1987, BLOC Development. It was the beginning but soon followed by several more due to cash I had on hand. A friend of mine at the time shared interest in technology and investing. So, he would funnel deals over to me in the after-hours and weekends. We'd chew the fat for hours over pasta at Anna's, burgers at the Apple Pan, or someplace for frozen yogurt in Westwood about the next greatest thing. We were getting high on tech, and it was fun and a welcome diversion from my real estate gig. We'd talk about our dreams and the places we'd visit and adventures we would have but never mentioned the money. It was never about that. It was like we were playing to have bragging rights and dreams.

It wouldn't be long before a handle full of those stakes matured into a payday or a pile of manure. And I had my share of both. I learned more from the losers than the winners, and all and all had a blast while it lasted. Eventually, I needed to liquidate my holdings to survive the Savings & Loan fiasco, and my friend soon left Los Angeles to find himself and greener pastures as he disappeared under a cloud of his firm's collapse.

Quite a few years passed until I was able to return in the mid to late nighties to experience the rise and fall of the tech boom. As I got educated about the operational side of the technology world, as well as valuations and exits, I learned lessons for a lifetime. I studied investments carefully and searched for the secret sauce and then concluded that at the macro point of view, the secret sauce was similar to other industries.

It was now a handful of years later, and with too many investments gone by to remember. I had been in and out of deals in various capacities and for different amounts. I had acquired an enormous amount of experience and knowledge that remained. It had grown exponentially, and now I was most proud of myself for becoming a discriminating and disciplined investor. It was as if I could see the holes in the paper even before reading a hopeless opportunity. On the flip side, my investing had eroded to a slither despite plentiful opportunities. It was a fine line, and the challenges came every day. However, I had many other things on my plate between existing businesses and my family to keep me from getting upset or deterred.

> The people that are crazy enough to think they can change the world are the ones who do.
>
> STEVE JOBS

The TV was broadcasting cartoons across the lengthy, expansive soaring-ceilinged family room that transitioned into the incorporated dining area and sleek contemporary open Italian kitchen. The kids scattered about the house lying on the creamy mocha sofa and in their rooms chatting with friends and tending to homework.

It was dinner time with the accent of the stainless-steel stove hood exhausting the effervescent aroma of the tasty lemon butter sauce awaiting its introduction to the paneed chicken. It was a cuisine concerto in full flow expecting its epilogue before arriving before its eager and beholden audience.

A glass of wine seemed in order and without notice, a cork extracted from a bottle of notable Silver Oak. "Dinner's ready," I exclaimed with a familiar ring tone emanating from the backdrop. "Someone has perfect timing," as I swung in the direction of the discord. "Hello, oh I'm putting dinner on the table may I call you later? Perfect!"

The kids flocked to their usual seats around the table. No one had a designated place, but somehow or another, everyone had their favorite spot. The dishes got plated up with fair portions for everyone. "Dad, don't forget the sparkling water," my son, the senior, shouted. "How about you help yourself with that while I get the plates on the table? I replied. "Girls first," as I slipped the first plate in front of my daughter. The rest delivered in sequence, and we were good to go. "Thanks for dinner," the kids said collectively. For the next hour, we relished the day's stories and savored another excellent meal. It was finally time to wrap it up, and we jointly cleared the table and retreated to our respective rooms.

"Oh, almost forgot, I promised Elena I'd call her after dinner" I picked up the landline and drew the receiver to my ear as I punched in the number. "Hey, Elena, sorry about before, but literally, I was sitting down with the kids for dinner," I explained. "Oh, don't be silly! I was calling you to ask a favor," as she giggled. "Sure, what is it?" Not thinking. I'd like you to meet my boyfriend, he's got something, something or other, I'm not exactly sure, but I think you would be very interested, but I can't explain it so would you meet with him for me? I'm sure you'll get what he's talking about." I have to say I was confused yet intrigued. Before I had time to think," Yeah, no problem, have him call me at the office tomorrow so we can arrange a meeting. For you, absolutely" "Oh, thank you so much, and again, I'm truly sorry for not being able to explain more. I'm certain you'll get it, and you'll like him too! Thanks so much and enjoy the rest of your evening."

It was a busy morning getting everyone off to school and then racing to the office for back to back meetings. I'd take the sessions in the large airy conference room adjacent to my office with phone calls interspersed. There wasn't time to leave for lunch, so I called Caesar and ordered my customary chopped grilled chicken Caprese salad and a bottle of sparkling Voss from il Tramezzino.

The food arrived within fifteen. It was unassuming Caesar himself stepping off the elevator into the foyer and peering through the glass window, followed with a waive, and a smile. "Mr. Keith, I have your food, and Veronique slipped in one of those cannoli you love to eat. Enjoy and have a good lunch!" "Terrific, I probably should take this next door to my office and have some privacy." I thought. And, so I did!

And BOOM! There it was sitting squarely in the middle of my black leather desk blotter lined with two gold bands on each side. It was a blotter I had for more than ten years. It was a gift for closing a deal and saw an incredible amount of action over those years. It was from an exquisite leather store in the center of town named Mark Cross.

The white message slip, you know the kind from Staples or Office Depot that is carbonless duplicates with the blue horizontal lines that come four to a page. The neatly inscribed message from the receptionist sat center with a telephone number and the name Tomás, "Elena's boyfriend." "Oh yeah, Tomás! So that's his name, I had forgotten to ask." I laughed. I thought this could be interesting? I can't imagine what he's got for me?"

I noticed the chocolate end dipped cannoli was peering out of the side of the brown plastic bag that had now relaxed on my desk. "Time for that Caprese" After all, I had my priorities, and if it wasn't the kids, food was next.

I shuffled around the desk and planted myself in my seat in starting position as if locked into the starting blocks for an Olympic sprint. I reached into the brown sack and pulled out of the clear plastic box that was housing my salad. I was addicted to this salad. I'd eat it at least three times a week. It was my concoction of a tomato and buffalo mozzarella salad with grilled eggplant and chopped grilled chicken piled to the maximum of the container with the balsamic vinaigrette quietly tucked on the side.

No time to waste! I popped the two-inch plastic top and slathered the dressing across the top, closed the salad lid, and grasped the edges firmly, and began shaking the box to-and-fro. Mixing the salad alone was a skill. Something, I mastered from having splattered too many white shirts with Veronique's balsamic. I expeditiously polished off the magnificent meal and relished the cannoli. And boy was it good, with the concluding bite being the ricotta and mascarpone cheese or something close to that at the end of the remaining crispy yet soft shell covered in chocolate. The final touch was the sparkling Voss to cleanse the palate and digestive track, a quick swipe of the remnants to clear my desk and back to work.

"Alright, Tomás, you're up!" I twisted to the left for the phone. Oddly enough on the left, I had a left-handed desk with the phone and computer on the left. I made the call and waited. Odd? I was right-handed, but when it came to particular tasks such as the phone or working on the computer, I was just more comfortable on my left. And so, I had the desk custom made from a substantial absolute black granite slab. It was known as absolute black granite because black granite is a factually black and gray speck, but absolute black granite is black-black with tiny gray, almost silver dots or speckles in it.

A few rings and then, clack, "Hallo?" "Hi, this is Keith Herman. I'm looking for Tomás." "Oh yes, yes, this is Tomás, nice of you to call," Tomás had an accent. It was a pleasant accent yet quite thick as he continued, where the conversation soon vanished.

I interrupted him, "Tomas! I'm very interested in what you have to say, but I have a meeting coming up and can't talk right now. I was calling to set up an appointment". I always found it best to quickly interrupt people I couldn't understand and make arrangements to meet. Otherwise, I knew I would become frustrated, unable to follow them on the phone. So, I interjected.

"Can you come to my office tomorrow afternoon so we can sit down without any interruptions?" "Perfect! Perfect!

Yes! Yes! Just tell me the time and where I will be there." "Come tomorrow afternoon at 4:00, and I will see you then." "Yes, see you then!"

Back to the conference room, I returned. My next meeting was in casual business attire, waiting patiently in one of the tall backed cream-colored chairs that sat on a stainless frame. A canvas satchel sat comfortably to the gentlemen's right on the conference table. He positioned himself to address the chair at the end of the table.

Human behavior always fascinated me and the etiquette of business and life. While appreciative of his intention to be respectful and placing me in the position of authority, I still found that things always went smoother when people were more at ease. I entered the room, where he stood to greet me. We shook hands, and I moved to the left. I passed on the opportunity for the end cap. Instead, I was now directly across from him and on even terms. I could see him exhale as if you had been relieved from military duty.

He was one of the entrepreneurs I met at The Beverly Hilton the day before. A very enthusiastic entrepreneur with a few endeavors under his belt looking for an investor for his next project. We chatted briefly and shared obligatory pleasantries before him getting to the main event.

Without further hesitation, he reached for his bag, and I presumed he was going for his computer. However, something else emerged from the tote. It was smaller, thinner, and sleeker than I anticipated.

"Have you seen one of these?" he asked. "No, what is it?" I inquired. "It's an iPad from Apple. I'll show you how it works."

It was genuinely captivating the more he shared the functionality with me. "Wow, a true convenience!" I said. "Yes, it is, now I'll show you my pitch deck that I have on here." he gloated.

And for the next several minutes, he shared his presentation. It was exciting but not even near as impressive as the iPad. I coaxed him to share with me any other projects he had, which I routinely did so that the meeting would not be a bust. We discussed a few more projects until we were interrupted by Mark, the office manager, who reminded me that I needed to go. We said our goodbyes and off I went to rendezvous with the kids for or usual evening.

I drove home quickly through the backstreets and up the mountain. I went through the private gate, down the winding road, and into the garage. Through the door and up the two half flights of stairs into the kitchen and it was game on. A quick assessment of the refrigerator and freezer and then polling of the kids for a final consensus.

How blessed I thought to be able to have that time and generally with few interruptions. And then, as if my thoughts revealed, my cell rings. "Hello!" "Hi Keith, it's Elena. I want to thank you for agreeing to meet with Tomás tomorrow. I very much appreciate it, and I know he's going to do something great." "Sure, no problem I'll talk with you later tomorrow."

She was uncharacteristically persistent, and I sensed the crazy fun person I came to know just, in fact, may have introduced me to something of real substance and potential. It was one of those odd, overwhelmingly moments of feeling something special. I allowed the moment to resonate fully and then transformed into Chef Keith for the next hour or so, getting dinner ready for our ritual dinner.

The evening passed, and then I was back to the grind. I was up, had my three-shot espresso, and then did the typical back and forth over the canyon to school and then to the office. I knew every twist and turn and could have traversed it blindfolded if necessary. It was roughly forty-five minutes each way, and we were either chatting about our previous night's dinner, the day's schedule, or studying for quiz or test. We passed the gates of the school and into the drop-off line and then back out to the street and headed for the canyon.

Time flew by consistently and miraculously. I was back at the office in no time flat and sitting at the helm sorting through the day's deals. They arrived daily via email and the US mail. The insatiable trashcan quickly consumed the memorandums and decks, and my email trash file was equally full. I commandeered anything with potential and placed it to the side of my desk in an obsessively neat pile.

Next, I took a few meetings, including one for lunch, with my calls sandwiched in between. The day was flying, and the office phone chirped once again.

"Hey Mark, you ring?" I joked. And very professional, he responded, "Quite funny, yes, your 2:00 pm appointment Tomás is here, shall I send him up to your office or one of the conference rooms?"

Mark had a great sense of humor but was professional to a fault. I couldn't help but laugh! "Have him come up to the large conference room next to my office" "Will do!" he said.

I straightened up my desk to not lose a beat for my return. I got out from behind the desktop, and it was five short paces to the door, a U-turn to the right, and seven quick strides to the conference with the swinging glass entry door to the room on the right.

I entered the room, and there was Tomás, sitting in the usual suspect's chair. "Hi, Tomás, nice to meet you!" "yes, nice to meet you too! He replied in his distinct accent. "Thank you so much for seeing me. Elena talks about you often and insists I meet you. She believes you can help me with my work."

"Well, I guess we'll find out," as I laughed. "First, tell me about yourself." I prodded. "Oh, me and Elena …. we are very much in love! I can't stop thinking about her even though I have known her for quite some time. Lucky, I have work I need to do, you know?" We both laughed.

He was a nice foreign chap, although hardly British. He was polite, average in stature, clean-cut, modestly dressed with absolute European confidence. The kind that was not overly confident yet not sheepish. He seemed very even-keeled, and happy go lucky with a particular familiar style and flair even in his modest attire.

He seemed genuinely sincere in his intentions and passionate about life and his work. All in all, I was quite relaxed in his presence and was glad to hear he was crazy for Elena. I had sensed her joy in our brief conversation a few nights prior and now understood why.

"So why don't you tell me what exactly you're working on Tomás?" "Oh yes, of course, yes, yes, and thank you again for taking the time to see what I have." "Certainly!" I said as he segued to his bag that obscured from my view.

I couldn't imagine what he had for me in that bag. It was always an adventure like when I was a little kid watching "Felix the Cat" on TV in the early weekend mornings as my parents slept. Felix had "a bag of tricks" as they called it, and you never knew what Felix, the black-cloaked white-faced puss, would be pulling out of his bag next.

Was it an entertainment project related to Elena? Or, a physical product he wants to show me? "What could it possibly be?" as I sat in suspense.

The flap swung back, and promptly a laptop materialized. Nothing exceptional for the time. Although, by today's metrics, it would have undoubtedly garnered a few chuckles. I didn't even think twice when Tomás popped the lid on that 17" baby.

Ironic, considering I had just been introduced to an iPad for the first time the day before that was a pittance in comparison with the same horsepower. He booted it up, and as he patiently waited for Mathilda to come back to life.

I ducked out to the nearby restroom just behind the elevators only a few yards from the conference room. I knew it would most likely be a long meeting, so this was now was my chance.

I quickly returned, and Voila! He was ready with the pitch. To this day, I have no idea whether it was the accent, language barrier, the pitch materials, or my inability to focus, but nothing made any sense. I let him finish out respect to Elena and then had the pleasure of being asked, "So, do you have any questions?"

Ah, yeah, I thought to myself, but what to do? I went back to my fail-safe and asked for a moment and closed my eyes, and relaxed. It must have seemed like an eternity to Tomás, but I needed it.

"Are you ok?" he asked. "Oh, yes! I just needed to clear my mind from some other things that were on my mind, so you have my full attention." "Thank you. You must like it." he blurted.

"Ok, so how about we forget about all the pitch stuff, and you just show me the technology?" And, with that, he worked his magic. Manipulating the computer to carry out some genuinely different tasks, it was poetry in motion; I was unquestionably dazzled.

It was now running late, and I needed to head out. "Tomás, great stuff, I like it! Can we meet again and discuss it further? Unfortunately, I need to leave now to be with my family, but I'm very interested in what you have."

"Oh yes, of course," he replied. "Next week, I come and show you more things; it will update it with things we are still working on." "Perfect," I said. Let me know which day, and we'll make it happen.

CHAPTER 10

The Beauty of Technology

IT WOULD BE A few days until Tomás would get back to me. In the meantime, I was having moments of simultaneous wonder and disbelief. His demonstration defied previously accepted general computing limitations. Nevertheless, I needed to get an adequate handle on the technology itself before coming to any conclusion, so we planned to meet specifically for that purpose.

The days in the interim were a total mind-bender as I struggled to imagine what the hell was happening on the backend of big old Mathilda. She was too seasoned to have any tricks up her sleeve, so there must be a simple explanation, I thought. At the same time, the monetization opportunities were plentiful and relentlessly pecked away at me.

The deals were still rolling in, and there was no shortage. However, with each one I scanned, I had Tomás' in the foreground. I even had a follow up with the entrepreneur from the Beverly Hilton with the iPad. He had now pitched me a few more projects, and one looked interesting. The wheels continued turning with Tomás in the limelight, but I wasn't going to let curiosity kill this cat. After all, I reminded myself that I was a seasoned and disciplined investor, and I was going to keep things calm, and that's that, push pause!

The day finally arrived, and no Tomás. We had a confirmed appointment for the same 4:00 pm slot at my office but no Tomás. The conference room was looking lonely, and after fifteen minutes past the hour, I decided to give him a ring.

I picked my cell phone off the conference room table and manipulated the number quickly to get a ringing as I glanced out the window. A few rings and, "Hello, Keith. I am late. The traffic is terrible. I'll be there in twenty minutes. Ok! Bye!"

From the halcyon view, my gaze dropped to the phone as if to find solace. I just shook my head and laughed as I brought my gaze back to center and contemplated the evening's dinner selection. Food was the default, and now I was getting hungry.

Before I could decide on dessert, Mark was calling to announce Tomás. "Hi Keith it's Mark, I have Tomás here in the lobby, shall I send him up to the large conference room?" "Yes, please! Thanks, buddy!"

Within a few beats, I could see through the floor to the ceiling glass pane of the conference room the stainless elevator doors retract, and an exasperated Tomás charge out. He possessed a focus, intensity, and determination I had yet seen. He was going to get to brass tacks, but we had a long way to go. Without understanding the "Amazing Mathilda," there would be no advance on any front.

"So sorry, I am late! The traffic was terrible, and I try my best to get here on time, but it was just terrible, terrible," "No worries, come and sit down and relax for a few minutes." As I spotted, he was a tad disheveled this time around. He was in his conventional attire, neatly pressed dark gray cotton slacks, and a relaxed dark-blue buttoned-down shirt that appeared to have shifted with the tide, so that is was now lying somewhat lopsided. He hadn't shaved, to my best guess, in perhaps five or six days, but it somehow suited him. And, his hair matched with a slight disarrangement to it.

"Tell me, how are things with you and Elena?" He gushed, "Oh, she's my love and light! I work like a madman I tell you and when I see her……" as he rambled on.

"Have some water and relax." I prodded. "Oh, thank you, thank you!" He rattled on about Elena and how he wanted to marry her and have a family. He was pouring his heart out as I'd never seen someone do before, and it was beautiful and inspiring. The passion and the clarity of his vision were a blockbuster romance movie in technicolor on the big screen before me. This guy knew what he wanted, and I had no doubt he would achieve it for better or worse.

He eventually settled in and reached for Mathilda, who had been patiently waiting next to him, like a child sitting next to their parent waiting to see the doctor. Except in this scenario, I was assuredly the doctor about to examine the patient before rendering a diagnosis.

He glided her out of the bag and lifted her lid onto the table. There she sat with a few pages of paper lying in the center of her belly. He placed his fingers on them to grab ahold and collectively pulled them towards himself, then flipping them over.

In his European accent and now clear as a whistle, he asked, "I hope you no mind, but we must sign a non-disclosure agreement for me to share the coding with you?" I am getting patents, and I must be sure I have protection. I know, no need to worry, you will take anything from me because you are Elena's good friend, but it's good business. Would you mind signing it for me?" "Not at all, I sign them all the time.' And with a quick swipe of my pen, it was done!

He then cranked her up, and once again, I reasoned it best to sneak in a restroom break. I quickly rebounded, and he was ready to go. "I want to tell you again, thanks for your interest and why I need your help."

Without a thought, I cut him off before he could get into the weeds. "I appreciate sharing this opportunity with me and all the details. I believe the best way I can help is if I can better understand exactly how the technology works. Do you mind if we start from there, and then we can go into the details and how I may be able to help?" "Of course," he said.

The adventure began, and, to be frank, I admittedly was undoubtedly skeptical. It was as if Tomás were taking me to meet the Loch Ness monster or Bigfoot. Something that others claimed to have seen, but I needed to see it with my own eyes.

If his creation was legit, the possibilities were limitless. He pressed on explaining the backend, meaning the coding, how it worked and integrated into other technologies. I was impressed and listened attentively to absorb as much as possible as he proudly shared his baby.

Before long, the presentation had ended, and there was a considerable amount to process. The coding had left me dizzy, and the possibilities were growing. My mind was swirling, but more importantly, I needed food!

"So Tomás, tell me how may I help you?" I offered. "Keith, I need several hundred thousand dollars investment for the project. I would like you to invest with me." He stared. "Okay, so tell me about the financial picture. What exactly do you need the money for, and what are your projections?" I responded.

The room went silent. From staring, Tomás had dropped his face into his lap like a bout of narcolepsy. "Was he upset? Was he lost with words to be translated? Was he just tired?" I couldn't imagine, but the pause became uncomfortable as I waited. The feeling that came over me was not an optimistic one. It was more a feeling of uncertainty or perhaps a lack of truth. Either way, it wasn't ideal.

"Keith, I am not a businessman like you!" he proclaimed. "Oh, this is not good!" I thought. "I am an inventor, and this is my invention. Keith, I need your help. You understand this and what can be done with my creation" Now it was my turn, I had lost my voice. Shades of Dr. Frankenstein and the Wacky Professor filled the void between my ears. What a dilemma? Time to put on the "Diplomat Hat."

With a deep breath, I leaned forward across the table and peacefully conveyed, "I would like to help you! I need to gather enough information to understand how I can help if I can help at all. Do you have a business plan or a financial statement, perhaps that you used for your taxes last year? What about the paperwork for the patents?"

"Ah, I understand, yes, yes, I have all that. I can give you no problem!" I was now very on edge and not my usual optimistic self, and I blamed it on hunger. I need to eat!

"Tell you what, get all your paperwork together, and then you can bring it to me to review. Fair enough?" I posited. "Yes, yes, I have it for you in a few days." He replied. "Terrific!" as he lured Mathilda back into his bag for a lightening exit to beat the traffic.

My curiosity was waning, my keen self was back crawling through piles of deals on my desk, and in my email folder. There were projects on the drawing board in VR (virtual reality), AR (augmented reality), SaaS (software as a service), wearables, like Fitbit, and so many other areas.

It was a matter of mass adoption and exponential growth. A handful looked very promising in VR, AR, wearables, and the mobile solutions space, so I committed to making that my focus. These were the areas that were percolating, and I felt it was the future based upon consumer and enterprise interest demand. It was the future, and I wanted to be a part of it.

I was soon on the trail of several promising opportunities. One deal, in particular, caught my eye. It involved AR, and the project team was based out of Norway and offered technology to revolutionize commerce.

The small, diverse group was an even mix of men and women that worked together seamlessly. They were joyous, playful, and fun to be around as they worked. They were already deep into the development and were getting traction but needed strategic fuel for their fire. They appeared to be a good fit.

Another opportunity revolved around a VR headset. There were also APP possibilities that included Dropbox, Hulu, Instagram, and Groupon. Even the entrepreneur that I had met at the Beverly Hilton had come up with something promising.

There wasn't enough time in the day to get everything done. First, it was the teaser of the project, typically three to five pages or slides that gave the broad picture and then the NDA (non-disclosure agreement). Once the NDA was out of the way, I would receive the full-on offering to review. I'd have a quick look and, if interested, would then research specific aspects of the offering.

Deals were plentiful, and time was short. And once again, Tomás was late. It hadn't dawned on me only because business was jumping, as well as countless opportunities. I was obsessed and intoxicated with all the cool new stuff. It was warm, tingling, and mind-altering and had me entombed in my computer.

The time mysteriously slipped away unrecognized. Unless or, until, I got a holler from Mark announcing a call, a guest, or, even more likely, the arrival of my lunch, I wouldn't budge until calling it a day to meet up with the kids.

"Hi Keith, it's Mark. I have Tomás in the lobby. Shall I send him up." "Yes, Mark! I'll meet him in the fourth-floor conference room."

I compulsively straightened my desk and got everything off the black blotter and into neat little stacks organized on the right side of the blotter in an overlapping graduated manner. It looked alluring to me like magazines or newspapers at the newsstand or in a waiting room. I couldn't constrain myself from picking one of them up. And the same holds for whatever sat on my desk. I knew it and was entertained by it. I'd giggled every time I caught myself in the midst of it, priceless! "Alright, let's see what this boy has for me!" And I departed for the conference room next door.

CHAPTER 11

Comedy Central

I'LL NEVER FORGET THAT conference table! It was the table I frequently sat at for more than fifteen years, entertaining all sorts of people. I'd even sit there at times when I was just bored with my office or wanted to stretch out. It was nearly the length of the room, perhaps fifteen feet long. An odd shape, they call it a boat shape because its curved on the sides, you know bowed outward, with flat ends. And the top, made of maple with a brilliant lacquer finish and black plastic compartments in the center to house the plug outlets for your computer or equipment to do slide presentations, as well as the conferencing phone. Yes, I'll never forget that conference table!

I pushed the glass door back to the right in an arc into the room and released it as I entered. I turned my head left and with a smile released a prominent "Hey, Tomás, how are you?" as he stood to greet me.

He was now sitting in a different chair than the usual suspects with his back to the floor to ceiling glass panes overlooking the city, instead of the waiting area. "I'm good, good, and how are you, Keith?" "I'm good, thanks for asking. What's going on with you guys?" as I took the seat across from him. "Oh, everything is fine." "We are delighted, and Elena, tell me to tell you hello." "She very much respects you and thinks much of you." "Well, when you get home, give her a big hug for me!" "of course, of course," he said.

"Well, here we are again," I said. "Yes, and again thank you so much for spending your time with me." He affirmed. "Well, that's what friends do, they help each other.," I said.

So, before we get started, would you mind sharing with me why you are working on this project. I know you enjoy your work, but I am not speaking to you now as Tomás the Inventor. You mentioned last time we spoke that you see yourself as an Inventor. Instead, I am talking to you as Tomás, the person. Do you understand? I'm interested to know how this project fits into your life with Elena and the future. You know what I mean?" And the response, the classic, "of course, of course."

"Keith, I tell you the truth," as he leaned into the table. I could see a transformation as his posture morphed, and he hunched forward, placing his arms on the table as he leaned into it. His face filled with color, and I could sense the adrenaline. It was passion! Passion on a whole other level! A fire, I had not seen in so long that it caught me altogether off guard and gave me goosebumps.

"I tell you I love everything I do. It's because I do the things that make me feel good. I give Elena all my attention when I am with her so she can be happy too. I want us to be happy and have a happy family one day soon. You know, children? And my work, the same. I work day and night with people halfway around the world, and I don't even care if I don't sleep. I want to do something to make people's lives easier and bring them happiness even if it is with something that they think is small; it doesn't matter. I want to bring happiness. It is what I am supposed to do. It is my life!" he confessed.

I sat quietly as his passion had now drifted him halfway across the table. WOW, this was compelling! I was speechless, inspired, energized as if he had given me his all. In the gap of silence, the passion dissipated, and he gently and gradually retreated, falling back in the plush high-backed cream-colored chair in exhaustion. And, softly spoke, "Keith, I need your help!"

I now saw Tomás in a new and different light. He was no longer Tomás, the Inventor. He had transformed into Tomás, the man of conviction, passion, desire, discipline, persistence, belief, and action all to achieve his destiny. He had more to him than I had seen any entrepreneur. I was impressed! I was now delighted and ripe to see the plan and the statements I had requested at our last meeting. I had a warm and fuzzy feeling!

"Tomás, genuinely, thank you so much for sharing that with me! I greatly appreciate you being so open about your life and your work. It was meaningful and helpful. I liked what you had to say and want to learn more about your project and hopefully help you. Why don't you reach into your bag and get me the papers I asked for, so I may learn more?"

He maneuvered from his collapsed position in the chair to his customary left. He appeared to hug the chair next to him. He fumbled for a New York minute and then slowly pivoted back to center with Mathilda in one grip and a box under his arm. I didn't think twice as he laid her down in front of him and the featureless box casually just off to her side. It was a plain box, Nothing fancy, no markings to attribute to a product or a brand.

"Okay, must be something he's just bought and is taking home or something he plans to return at a store. Let's get to the numbers," I thought. The lid came open, and Mathilda was firing up. I tried not to be impatient, but as I caught a glimpse, I could see there were no papers in her belly this time around.

"So Tomás, do you have the operating statements for me in your bag, or on your computer?" "Uh, Keith, what do you mean about these operating statements you keep talking about?" in his distinct dialect. I asked the accountant, and he said, we don't have any operating statements."

With a quick snap of my neck and an exalting heart rate, I was fortunate enough to hook my eyes before they departed my skull. For real? I reiterated silently. "For real? For real? Just breathe, breathe, let it pass, let it pass." I coached myself.

"Tomás, I asked you if you filed taxes for the business, and you said yes. So, you must have some numbers for me to take a look at, no?" "Ah, yes, we did file our taxes, but those statements are not operating statements the accountant told me."

It was not a good sign! I could see this conversation was heading for circles, like an Abbott & Costello comedy routine.

Abbott: I say, Who's on first, What's on second, and I Don't Know's on third.
Costello: Are you the manager?
Abbott: Yes.
Costello: You going to be the coach too?
Abbott: Yes.
Costello: And you don't know the fellow's names?
Abbott: Well, I should.
Costello: Well, then who is on first?
Abbott: Yes.
Costello: I mean the fellow's name.

> **Abbott:** Who.
>
> **Costello:** The guy on first.
>
> **Abbott:** Who.
>
> **Costello:** The first baseman.
>
> **Abbott:** Who!

However, this situation with Tomás was now hardly entertaining! "Okay, Tomás, can you show me the tax returns for the business? Or, possibly, there could be a one or two-page document within your returns that has the information. Are they on your computer, or are they in your bag? Or, do you have some statement that shows the money you spent each year for the past few years broken down into categories?"

"Oh yes, yes, of course, I brought you numbers and everything you need, just like you ask.", with a glint in his eye. And without hesitation and in slow motion with a Cheshire grin on his clean-shaven face, he proudly tilted his head downward at the undistinguished box, put his hand behind it, gazed at me and gracefully began sliding it toward me across the glistening maple finished tabletop. The unambiguous gritty echo of the leisurely accelerating box reverberated as I observed with befuddlement. It skimmed along until it came to rest within less than an arms-length of me.

"What is this?" abandoned my lips as I looked him square in the eyes. "It is everything you asked me to bring! It's all there!" With angst and the gentle swaying of the head, he could not have been prouder!

"This is a shoebox!" I declared. "Tomás, is this a joke? Is something going to pop out when I open it?" "Ah, ha-ha! Keith, you ask me for everything! It's there, in the box!"

I could not imagine this to happen. I had spent decades looking at all sorts of opportunities and dealing with all kinds of people, but this was an absolute first. A SHOEBOX!

I peered at the box and then cradled it to draw it closer. I brought it within inches of me, sitting it lengthwise and removed the lid, placing it on the table behind the box. I stared into the bowels of the box. Paper! All sorts of paper! Small pieces of paper, medium sizes of paper, large sheets of paper, crumpled papers, folded papers!

My head began to wobble. I snatched the crooked piece of paper that sat atop the pile and turned it over. I positioned it in my hand for closer analysis. It resembled something from an old-time adding machine tape. I could see numbers in faint gray on the white paper torn from a roll. I looked closer.

Sushi! It was a receipt for Sushi! I shifted back to the bowels and grabbed the next piece of paper atop the pile. This one was roughly three times the size of the first, and upon examination could see that it too was a receipt. This time, Indian food. WTF?

"Tomás, what the hell did you bring me? These are food receipts for sushi and Indian food!" "ha ha ha, oh yes, yes, I brought you everything. That is everything we spent, even food. You need to look more in the box; you will find what you need,"

I foraged through the papers as if I was trying to pick the winning ticket to a drawing. I finally captured something of substance. I was not much bigger than a deck of cards, but it had depth, about a third the thickness and a bit longer. And, it was mangled and twisted as if a piece of discarded garbage.

I brought it to the surface and took a close look, a checkbook! An old twisted checkbook. I pried it apart and floundered through it, attempting to view the handwritten entries.

It was going nowhere! I thought. As much as I liked helping people, this didn't seem to be one of those instances. I needed clarity on more than just the technology. As much as I was impressed with Tomás' passionate plea, it had seemed that we were now at an impasse.

I was a disciplined investor, and numbers ruled in my world. Without them, it all seemed hopeless. Had it not been for Elena, Tomás would have been long gone and forgotten, amidst the sea of deals flowing through my mail and inbox. It was a problem! I needed a break!

"Tomás, I have another meeting coming up shortly, so why don't you tell me what's in the box for now, and I will have a look through everything later. "Ah, yes, well, everything is in there you need, the expenses and some legal papers, don't' worry, it's all there, it's all there," he said with conviction.

It was clear I wasn't going to get what I had hoped for, so we said our goodbyes. "I'll get back to you on this once I get through everything. Just be patient and give me some time and give Elena my best regards!" "Yes, of course," as he shuffled onto the elevator. I then returned to the conference room to fetch the shoebox on the way back to my office.

A week would pass as the plain lonely shoebox sat atop a tall black, five-foot-tall, five drawer lateral filing cabinet with brushed chrome handles in the back corner of my office behind my desk. It was one of several black cabinets and filled with deals that had gotten done. NDAs, memorandums, due diligence materials, and contracts were anchored within legal-sized manila folders and stored away while the failed transactions exited with the trash. The shoebox had somehow escaped the grasp of the cleaning lady and silently stood fast atop the cabinet.

Upon my arrival one morning, my assistant inquired about the mysterious box. I had forgotten about the shoebox, and with no reminders from Tomás or Elena, so there it sat. "So, what's up with the shoebox in your office?" she inquired. "New pair of shoes', as she giggled.

She knew I had a thing for shoes. "Well, not exactly," I replied. The curiosity was overwhelming to her. She already snuck a peek and knew more or less of the contents. She couldn't figure out why I would let it rest there. After all, I had a compulsion to put everything away or in plain sight for me to deal with timely. It was an exception, and it was tickling away at her.

"I need you to do something for me!" I confessed. "Sure, what do you need?" "I need you to take the box and sort everything out into piles so I can figure out what's there. Just do your best, and I'll take it from there." I said. "Done!" and off she went to sort through the contents.

By days end, she completed the task and left the shoebox, along with a few neat piles of different dimensions, sitting upon my desk. I threw the stacks into separate manila folders and gingerly dropped them into my soft briefcase. I toted them home and figured I have a look at them over the weekend when I could steal some time.

The weekend came, and I awoke early one morning. The kids were all still fast asleep as I climbed the short stairs to the kitchen to grab my customary morning triple espresso. With the push of two buttons, I was set and retreated to my room, where I spotted the files upon my dark stained bamboo desk in the far corner of the room.

Curiosity had now gotten to me. I figured what the heck let's have a look at what's there. To my surprise, aside from a considerable amount of petty receipts, I could see there were, in fact, some legitimate legal documents and several check registers. The legal documents would require some concerted time to read and research, so I took a swing at the check registers.

My accountants had handled my banking needs, and I paid for everything with cash or credit cards. I had not seen a check register for years except for an electronic record in Quicken and QuickBooks that I used to reconcile a few minor accounts. It was like visiting the museum, a blast to the past. The whole thing seemed altogether silly, but I was curious to see what they had been spending more than a half-million dollars doing.

The more I burrowed into the first book, the more curious I became. At first glance, it appeared that many of the entries were to the same payee and so I thought perhaps it might not be too challenging to segregate the payees at least. I got on my trusty 17" black Sony Vaio laptop from my briefcase and opened up an Excel spreadsheet. I did everything in Excel. I learned how to use Lotus123 back in the day and then taught myself Excel spreadsheets. I lived and died by them. I knew if I could get the data organized, I could quickly manipulate into all sorts of things. The game was on!

Within a short period, I realized it wasn't going to be so easy after all. There were far more payees than I envisioned and several books to rummage through. So, I moved to plan B. I delegated it out.

It would be roughly another week until I received the raw file in my hands. I worked the data and prepared it for the next steps. It involved getting invoices and any other documentation available for clarity on the payees. I didn't have much hope on obtaining any more documents such as invoices, etc. but I was looking for a reasonable amount of clarity on the finances.

I dialed up Tomás and explained the situation, and he walked me through the payees and information the best he could. From there, I created financial statements and balance sheets and low and beheld they appeared to mirror what Tomás had recalled from memory. I was now somewhat optimistic, so I gave Tomás a ring.

"Hey Tomás, how are you?" "Ah, Keith, Keith, nice to hear from you. I am good, good! Do you have good news for me?" "Well, I have all your numbers in order, and I would like to discuss them with you and the money you are looking for investment. Can you come to the office tomorrow in the late morning?" "Ah, yes, of course, I will be there at 10:30! I see you then!" "Terrific, see you then," We were all set to go, and I was looking forward to seeing Tomás this time around to obtain the remaining answers to a handful of outstanding questions.

The clock hit 10:30 am, and once again, no Tomás. He was a walking paradox. Impossible to set your watch by him. Either Europeanly fifteen to twenty minutes late or prompt as could be. He was a man of passion, and his tardiness was never an expression of his seriousness. Everything was serious! Time management was just not his thing, the typical inventor! This time a text! I will be there in 10 minutes, as I looked at the time on my phone, already 10 minutes late.

An exact 20 minutes late! "Hi Keith, it's Mark. I have Tomás here in the lobby." "Great, send him up" I captured the shoebox like a football, tucked it under my arm, and rushed to the conference room.

No sooner than I hit the soft conference room chair facing the elevator through the glass-paneled wall, Tomás stepped off the elevator. He was winded, unshaven, his dark brown hair indistinguishable from his beard and hair ostensibly tousled.

No wave hello, no more props only him and Mathilda. A straight shot into the room! "Keith, Keith, perfect timing!" he shouted with a smile.

He was thoroughly agitated and needed soothing. "Tell me about your weekend with Elena." I diverted him. "Oh, terrific news, terrific news, I tell you! We are getting married."

"That is excellent news! I said. "Yes! Yes! Yes!" He exclaimed. "We spent the weekend driving around enjoying each moment as we often do." I could see serenity overcome him and watched him sink into the seat across from me. It was time to press on.

"Tomás, I want to share the statements that I created and talk about the money you want and how you will use it." "Ah, very good, very good! I tell you whatever you need!"

I moved to the head of the table for better positioning and slid the statements cattycorner for us to review together. I began rolling down the line items and quickly done. 'Okay, so what do you need to know? He asked. "I need to know why half of the money you spent didn't go into the business."

"Well, Keith, I tell you, I have an equal partner, but the partner invested half the money, but he did this, and he did that, and he didn't do this," and on and on and soon, everything transitioned to black! "I get it, it's not pretty, but I get it.

So, tell me how you will use the money?" I inquired. "I will get rid of my partner!" with a big smile. I sprung awake! I was wonderstruck! What did he mean and why he would give money to his partner who invested half the money but spent half the dough with most probable impropriety? Why would he be entitled to any money?

An evil thought had passed my mind! "Tomás, how will you get rid of your partner? What exactly do you mean?" "I will pay him to go away, and that is that!" "How much?" I asked. "I will give what you give me, and that is that," he said.

Nothing was making sense at this point. Tomás needed money to finish the development of the technology and to secure certain patents and for other expenses. Where would that money originate?

I said to him, "Tomás, what you have is more than invention. You have potentially the foundation for a very profitable business." "Keith, I know I have something compelling, something that could make a massive difference to people, something that can change the world of technology. I know I will do this! I need you to invest with me!

I had now reached the end of the rope. Tomás was all over the place, and nothing was coming together. I had invested a considerable amount of time and resources, and it was all out of a friendship. However, the business person in me declared it was time to extricate myself from this craziness. I couldn't imagine dealing with the uncertainty, and I sensed there was even more uncertainty than I had already witnessed. It was just time to bail.

"Tomás, you are asking me for almost a half-million dollars, and that is a tremendous amount of money for me. I am afraid I can't see how I will ever get the money back. You have no existing business, unfinished technology, no patents, no financial projections, and you will need more money. I'm afraid I can't give you the money.

However, I will still help you." "You will?" in surprise. "Yes, Tomás, I consider you and Elena good friends, and I would like to see you succeed. I will give you all the financial statements that I created and go over them with you again until you understanding them and how to use them. And, and I will help you with a pitch deck so that you may approach someone else to give you the money. Hopefully, it will get you where you want to go."

I was now relieved. "Thank you, thank you, I understand and thank you for helping me!" It was apparent to me that Tomás had technology that had tremendous potential.

However, it was very questionable whether or not he could see it to the conclusion of the development. If so, could he get it adequately protected with patents and then capitalize on it to reap the rewards ultimately? In short, it seemed extremely doubtful.

Looking back on the elements I had learned about success. I felt Tomás, in most probability, was not aware or conscious of the numerous challenges before him and with good reason. He had no prior experience in this arena whatsoever either on the technology side or business side. He boasted at times on the scale and magnitude of his creation, that may have been an expression of his Desire, Motivation, and Belief, but I perceived it as perhaps just his lack of experience and being unrealistic.

His articulated Plan included replacing his partner and finishing the technology. He said he then wanted to get it into the hands of everyone. It certainly was altruistic but was a nebulous Plan and did not include a specific course of action to accomplish it. Without this Plan and a Plan to address the financial picture, it seemed to me that even if he did have the funds, he was requesting, his Actions may not be sufficient. I couldn't afford the loss; it was now time to move on.

Nevertheless, I wanted to honor one of my life's valuable lessons and leave him in a better position than when I found him. It is why I offered him the financial statements and my assistance with a pitch deck. He was a quality person, and

I genuinely wanted to see his project have a better chance at success for both his benefit and Elena's and perhaps help him realize a life-long dream. It was akin to Clifton "Pop" Herring, who rejected Michael Jordon from his High School basketball team. Pop didn't just reject Michael, and that was the end of the story. He kept him on the junior varsity team and worked with him, so when the time came, he was ready to advance.

Within a day or two of our meeting, I heard from Tomás, "Hey Keith, I have questions about the papers and numbers. I want to understand you, will you help, no?" "Of course, let's go over them, and I will explain to you the terms. You know, the accountant's language or the names they use to sound impressive. It will help you, and you will sound more knowledgeable when you meet potential investors." "Ah, Keith, thank you!" In gratitude, "Thank You!"

I spent time with him reviewing the statements in considerable detail. We touched on the purpose of the various reports, why certain expenses appeared in specific sections, costs included & omitted, terminology (such as EBITDA, non-recurring charges, depreciable assets), and so on forth. It was an education for him and also rewarding for me.

Within a short few weeks, I get another call. "Hi Keith, it's Tomás. May I come, see you at your office." In an erratic tone. Something was amiss. In his brief request, his once familiar voice had slackened and faded with his accent now illusive. A certain bleakness had taken over as if he were in the dumps, gloomy, depressed, perhaps worried. I wasn't exactly positive.

"Are you okay? Everything alright?" "Oh, yes, of course, Keith, of course. May I see you tomorrow? I will take you to lunch. You must eat. I'll take you to lunch. I'll be there at 1:00, ok with you?" "Yes, Tomás, you sure everything is okay?" I asked cautiously. "Oh, yes! Oh, yes!" And, then click, he was gone! Not a good feeling, but I reminded myself I did offer, so lunch it is.

There were now a handful of deals that had me knee-deep. They had me beyond the offerings and satiated in research. They were different tech sectors, and it was task challenging. Time was also now a premium, and dodging out for lunch was not my choice. However, I gave him my word.

A glint out of my left eye, and it was the tiny blue neon light on the right-side edge of my black phone that indicated an incoming call. In an instant, it would ring! Above the little blue light lay the gray LCD strip displaying the time, 12:45 pm! The phone sounded, and I lifted the handle. Before getting the receiver to my ear, I heard a sunny, "Hi Keith, its Mark. I have Tomás here in the lobby. Shall I send him up?" 12:30? He's never been this early! And, a half-hour early. Oh, boy! I thought. "No, no, I'll be down shortly, tell him just to wait there." "Will do!" with a click.

It was of importance, but not a priority, so I pressed on as my priorities dictated. I finished off what I was doing and stacked the deals in perfection on the right side of the black blotter in order of highest to lowest and headed out.

"Hey Tomás, ready for some lunch?" as I came off the elevator. I surmised he hadn't slept in days. Again, unshaven beard, tousled hair, and this time his light blue eyes interred behind two elongated black bands stretching beneath them.

Admittedly, I felt uncomfortable and apprehensive about the conversation to come. "Yes, Keith, always a good meal! Shall we go?" Off, we went down the street to il Pastaio for a most needed glass of Amarone and Garganelli to settle things down.

We entered the restaurant and got seated toot sweet. The Amarone hit the table in moments, and with a few pleasantries and swigs, I was as calm as a cucumber.

"So Tomás, what's the matter?" "Oh, Keith, I have been working day and night with the developers to get everything working correctly. They are such idiots!

They keep me up all night with the miscoding all the time, and for them, it's their daytime, such idiots I tell you! But that is not the problem! The problem is I am going to run out of money, and I need to have that presentation, pitch, and numbers together so I can get money. Can you help me?

I know you have done so much already. I am so grateful I need this help because I know I will get the money. I do not know how or who, but I see it as I see my future with

Elena, the family, a happy life! I see it! I see it! Please, help me! Please!

WOW! It was a sobering moment! I am confident he does see all of what he described, but I can't imagine this is the path? This guy is up to his neck in manure, and he's counting on me? I can't even imagine that even with my help, he will get the money he is looking for or any money for that matter. There are way too many moving pieces and troubling questions to answer to an investor.

All common sense had left the restaurant, and before I knew what happened, the following rolled off my tongue, "Sure, I'll put everything together and in an easy manner for you to explain. Hopefully, you will be able to avoid the majority of the questions that came to my mind. I'll have it for you within a couple of days. If that's ok?"

Looking back, I fault the Amarone for allowing me to speak my truth. "Oh Keith, thank you, thank you, thank you so much!" he said with all sincerity. "Not to worry, let's enjoy the lunch, shall we? And Tomás, why don't you fill me in on the wedding plans?"

The truth, his situation resonated with me, and the Amarone, oddly enough, brought me clarity! I couldn't deny what I knew, we are all Conscious of our Destiny to a certain degree, and it's just a matter of moving beyond the fear of uncertainty to realize it.

Tomás was sure this was his Destiny, and nothing was going to stop him. I admired him and also believed this to be his Destiny; it was whether or not he would succeed is where I had my doubts. Like the many people that had helped me along the way, it was now my turn to pay it forward, and so I went home that evening and worked on the presentation deck.

I wasn't too concerned about getting the deck done as promised. I was confident since I had already completed more than a hundred for my ventures and perused several thousand for potential investments over the years. The question became how best to compile it so Tomás would feel confident explaining it and how to avoid a likely litany of explanations best.

The art is in the dance, and the choreography decided. It was now time for Tomás to practice before taking the floor. I invited him back to my office, where we sat for an afternoon going over various scenarios until he was convinced, he was good to go. There was nothing left for me to do other than wish him well as boarded the elevator. It was now a face-off with Father Time!

I was immediately incorporated back into the medium of deals and now pressing forward as I focused my sights on a handful of the projects. It was an exciting time, and fall was in the air with Muse Resistance Tour and Roger Waters, The Wall approaching. I was keeping long hours as I was now traveling and fielding questions from cities around the globe. Every day was a new adventure filled with learning new things, meeting new and exciting people, and addressing challenges to close a few winning deals. Months had passed without a word from Tomás and not even a peep from Elena until a most unexpected call!

CHAPTER 12

Off to the Races

"HELLO KEITH, ITS TOMÁS! How are you? It's been a long time." "I'm well, Tomás, nice to hear from you. How are things with you and Elena? "

Ah, Keith, thank you for asking! We are still in love, very much in love and planning the wedding. I can hear the bells. Elena! Hahaha, But, yes, everything is wonderful, and I have good news!"

"Wonderful, are you two having a baby?" I joked. "Ah ha-ha, not quite yet, but hopefully soon! No, I got the money!" he said.

"What money is that? I asked. "Keith, I got the money, all the money, and more! I used the statements and the deck, and I get twice the money. Can you believe it?" in a joyous tone.

"I was discombobulated! "What exactly are you talking about" I probed. "Oh, Keith, I tell you. I still cannot believe it myself! I met a man, an older man, a brilliant man that is retired with a lot of money and I told him about my invention, and he asks if he can be a part of it.

I didn't even ask him for the money. He tells me if you need money, I will loan you money, and you pay me back with some interest. Can you believe it, Keith? I got the money! It's already in my account. I want to thank you for all your help! Thank you, Keith! Thank you!"

I was aghast, it was surreal, and I felt something between disbelief and joy. Yet, I wasn't exactly 100% surprised. "Tomas, that's great news! I am so happy you got the money and enough to keep working, terrific! I shouted. "Yes, thank you again, Keith, and I will be in touch."

Luck? Fate? Destiny? Does it even matter? Everyone has their point of view. But, for the meantime, Tomás was still on his course, and there was no denying that.

Since we first met, he undoubtedly had a precise bearing in mind, no different than a sailor at sea for weeks with nothing but ocean surrounding him, yet sure of his course and destination. He had his mission, believed in it, and nothing would deter him. He worked tirelessly and endlessly without making excuses and was grateful for all the help along the way. He had just pulled off what most people would call the impossible or a miracle. Yet, he still was a long way from shore.

Tomás did have a long way to go, and I was genuinely happy for him. After all, he and Elena were soon to be happily married, and he was always very appreciative of the help. I also enjoyed the conversations and the friendship that developed. I knew the most significant challenges were ahead of him, and I was silently rooting for him.

He was a self-proclaimed inventor with no clear plan other than to complete the development of the technology. Beyond that, there was nothing. It was merely one step at a time in the blinding snow. It was unquestionably going to be an eyeful.

Months past and the technology sector became tempestuous. The wearables deal died due to patent disputes, and the VR deal headed south over an internal disagreement on company direction. It was challenging enough to get technology built and funding, and then you had situations with disputing founders over nothing more than egos. It was nucking futs! However, there were still some promising APPs, and the mobile solutions deal in the air with a reason for hope.

Wednesday came, and it was a La Scala day that meant a freshly baked Genzano bread, mixed green salad, and pasta, but not just any pasta!

"Hi Keith, its Mark. Your lunch delivery is here. Shall I send him up?" "Is the Pope Catholic?" I replied. The food arrived as my blotter transformed into a placemat. I quickly closed the door and with good reason. The aromas were permeating the flimsy white plastic bag holding the goods and overtaking the airspace.

The bag disappeared in a flash, and the room was now officially filled to the hilt. I popped the lid, and the veal Bolognese brought my teeth to life as I sported a ridiculous guilty grin. The salad was then exposed as I slipped the napkin into my shirt. It was time to dig in!

"Bdddt, Bdddt," sounded the phone. "Seriously," I thought. "I'm about to eat here!", "Hello," without taking an eye off the Bolognese. "Hi Keith, its Mark. I have Tomás on the phone." "Alright, put him through."

Hey Tomás, I'm just about to eat my lunch, what's up?" "May I come to see you in a couple of hours?" he asked. "Well, I'm short on time," I replied. "It won't take long, I promise. Just a few minutes of your time," he said. "Alright, fine, just swing by for a few minutes." I wasn't taking any more chances. So, I left the phone off the hook and returned to my feast.

"Bdddt! Bdddt!" "Hey Mark, send him up!" "I take it, you were expecting him," said Mark with a snicker. I dashed out to meet Tomás at the elevator and walked him into the conference room to save time.

"Ah, Keith, thank you so much for seeing me." "Yeah, Yeah, So, what's up, Tomás?" "Keith, I will soon be done with my invention. What do you suppose I do with it?" "I'm sorry, what exactly do you mean?" I replied. "I mean, how can I get it to everyone?" he asked. My invention? You know, so everyone uses it?"

"Tomas, seriously? Why couldn't you ask me something simple?" as I chuckled. I was neck-deep into a half dozen other deals, and the idea of diverting my focus to his "invention" was challenging.

"Ah, let me think!" I declared. I closed my eyes and let the thought simmer. "Well, from my experience, I would recommend a strategic partner! A partner that can distribute your invention to everyone, so you don't have to do the work. You know."

"Oh yes, that's a great idea!" he shouted with a smile. "Who," he asked. "Ahh, perhaps someone like a major software firm such as ……." and I rattled off a few names. "That's what you should do!" I said. "Hmmm," brilliant Keith, very smart, I like that! Thank you! I'll let you go back to work now." And off he went.

In hindsight, I didn't even think twice about the advice I gave Tomás. I may have put him at risk. The names I threw out were significant firms, and while it was tough to get through to the right person, it was also risky because many were known for taking technology for themselves regardless of issued patents. Nevertheless, it was water under the bridge, and I needed to get back to my deals that required my attention.

> "Many of life's failures are people who did not realize how close they were to success when they gave up."
>
> THOMAS EDISON

For the months that followed, unbeknownst to me, Tomás was spending his days and nights attempting to get a hold of a strategic partner, as I had suggested. He was giving it his all. He was going to conferences, networking events, and even making calls directly to companies, leaving message after message only for them to go ignored.

It was nowhere near as easy as he had imagined. And, it turned out neither was the development of his project. The oversees developers had been making errors left and right, and he had been flying back and forth, halfway across the globe to get his project concluded. He was now once again running low on funds, and there was the real reason for concern.

However, Tomás was determined to succeed. His true Belief was that his Destiny was to deliver something of value to many people to affect their lives. His Desire and Motivation were driving him to live up to his Values. It appeared that his Plan was deficient because even with all the Action he was taking, he was still coming up short of Success. What could be wrong? The window for opportunity seemed to be closing because funds were running out, and without real interest in his invention, how would he ultimately raise more money?

Tomás was anything but a gambler. He didn't believe in chance, he believed in Destiny. Ironically, as his life would have it, Tomás found himself going to Las Vegas on the spur of the moment adventure to a rather small and obscure technology conference. He didn't know anyone going to the meeting and had no leads.

It was just an excuse to escape work, family, and the overwhelming pressure that had accumulated over the years and was now bearing down on him. He decided on the long way and found himself driving across the hot and near barren landscape for hours. His isolation became his solace as he reflected on his journey while softly listening to his carefully selected playlist, including Mozart, Beethoven, Vivaldi, Strauss, Bach, Puccini, and more.

He pulled up to the affluent Wynn Hotel in his modest dust-laden rental car, opened the door to the oppressively hot arid air, and exchanged the keys for a ticket with the valet. As he entered the lobby, a greeting came by a wave of fresh, crisp cold air that reminded him of the thermoclines of life. Perhaps today was meant to be like any other day? Maybe it was just to be enjoyed?

He pressed on to the gallery hosting the event where folks were mingling about and helped himself to some coffee before taking a seat. He sat for the next few hours listening to banal presentations of insignificance and soon broke for lunch.

It was time to check in with his love Elena as he hit speed dial on his cell. No answer! "Hello, my dear. I am here at the conference. Not much is happening here, and I am now going to have some lunch. I'm thinking about you and hope you are enjoying your day. I will talk with you later, my love." and slipped the phone into his upper jacket pocket.

He made his way to the nearest café and was soon seated where he chose his favorite niçoise salad with iced tea and checked his phone for the latest news. As he scanned the discouraging headlines, two gentlemen were seated beside him. They were foreigners like him yet from the other side. Yes, opposite ends of the world.

"Hello!" Tomás politely spoke. "May I ask where you are from?" "Yes, we are from China. And you?" they replied. "I am from here, the US. I moved here from Europe several years ago."

They continued to converse about their personal lives and soon discovered a common interest in music, theater, and culture. "And, what do you do for work?' they asked Tomás. "I am an Inventor, and you?" "We are executives with a major Chinese company called _____. Perhaps you have heard of it?"

Oh Yes, Tomás most certainly had! It was one of the most well-known technology companies in the world, and they just so happen to be two of the top executives. Tomás could not resist. He mentioned his project, and they listened attentively, soon exhausting their time with Tomás' work. "

Are you here for the conference?" Tomás inquired. "No, we are here for other business, but we very much like what you have and would like to speak further." one of the gentlemen replied. Tomás was over the moon! They hastily handed Tomás their Business cards and asked him to call them to discuss his project further, and then they graciously parted ways.

Elated Tomás returned to the conference hall to finish out the otherwise uneventful day before leaving. He stepped out into the motor court to retrieve his rental, handed the valet his ticket, and lingered around reflecting on his lunch with the two gentlemen and their interest in his invention. A guilty smile filled his face as he perceived victory to be near. He was envisioning his design in full swing and glory, hearing the praise of many and the chills resonating throughout his body. He could smell and taste the sweetness of success. It was finally within his reach.

As the gentlemen requested, Tomás was shortly in touch, and their enthusiasm had not diminished one iota. The gentlemen disclosed their interest to work side by side with Tomás to bring his invention to life, and Tomás could not have been more satisfied. They painted a picture of cooperation and collaboration in every sense. They would even provide him with all the resources he needed to improve the product further. There was only one caveat. In return for all the assistance, Tomás would assist them in the development of a project that they had already produced, but needed improvement and they knew Tomás was genius enough to make it happen.

Through subsequent conversation, they eventually arrived at an agreement and entered into a partnership to first complete their project and then would proceed to put the finishing touches on Tomás' masterpiece. It could not have been any better.

Tomás called me to share the splendid news. "Hello Keith, this is Tomás, and I have great news. I entered into a partnership with the _____ Company! Can you believe it? They will shortly be my partner, and they will distribute my invention to everyone all over the world. Can you believe it?" he boasted. "Tomás, that's terrific! I'm happy your dream is coming true. Congratulations!" "Thank you, Keith! Thank you!"

Tomás' Plan had worked like a charm! He had a Conscious thought and perceived it to be his Destiny. It aligned with his Beliefs and Values, and his Desire became overwhelming to the point that his Motivation drove him to move forward one step at a time continually.

His Plan may not have appeared to be a Plan at all to others; for Tomás, it was the extent of his Planning. And it included continually asking for help along the way to achieve the next step, He never questioned it, he just went with it and took the best Action in each moment because he believed it would lead him to his Destiny.

Most notable, Tomás remained Conscious to continually evaluate his challenges, Plan, and Action and made adjustments as necessary. Just as Michael Jordan. He now had everything aligned and the partnership, like the winning Chicago Bulls, to grease the wheels to success.

Tomás would soon see the finish line. All that was left was to finish off a handful of tasks that were a piece of cake for Tomás, and he would finally realize his dreams after the many hard years of work. The sky was the limit. He would eventually have his championship ring!

The days past and the perfect June day arrived. The scattered natural light presented the sublime blue sky accompanied by the bouquet of roses.! Tomás and Elena were ripe with their vows, and the celebration would be noble and lavish. Not a detail missed as Elena had been planning this day for years.

The expansive lush bright green lawn that sat before the rose gardens lay meticulously groomed. The aroma of freshly manicured green blades competed with the roses. The Dual Layer Chiffon Altar gently waved to the guests as they ushered past to their high backed white lined seats to notable classics of Tomás' playlist.

The women sat with anticipation as the bride sat somewhere in the wings. The groomsmen stood in formation, awaiting their counterparts as the minister sailed to the altar for last-minute measures. It was truly remarkable as these two loving people were soon to be joined in matrimony and commence a joyous life, filled with love, happiness, leisure, beauty, and good fortune.

The ushers completed their duty, and the groomsman and bridesmaids arrived in perfect formation with the groom and bride soon to enter. Tomás made a grand entrance donned in a classic black tuxedo resembling Carey Grant. And Elena in her vibrant white gown with a cascading five-foot train. Everyone sat in awe as Elena and her father walked along the red carpet to the altar to meet with Tomás. The men briefly shared a brief handshake and embrace, and the ceremony commenced.

As the sunset in the distance, they exchanged their vows, and with a kiss, they were one. They finally did it, and now it was time to celebrate. The rice flew, and the champagne began flowing. The guests abruptly abandoned their chairs to mingle on the lawn with the new Mr. and Mrs. Congratulations was in abundance, and there wasn't a care in the air. And why should there? It was a fairytale story with a fairy tale wedding as everyone knew from the groom there was an excellent fortune forthwith as he had alluded.

The night raged on with tears of sorrow, tears of joy, and tears of laughter. A communion, to be cherished and remembered as new family and friends were united for an evening never forgotten. The extravagant event cycled through the various courses until it extinguished at dawn.

Mr. and Mrs. Tomás had now concluded their honeymoon days of basking in luxury and the afterglow. The honeymoon was a success, and Tomás was now prepared to take the helm. It would be smooth sailing from here, and he was anxious to cap off his years of hard work and see his invention transform the lives of the many as he had always dreamed.

First things first, it was time to check in with his partners. Tomás received a gracious and cordial welcome from his new partners. They were also extremely anxious and had been awaiting his return from his honeymoon to get the ball rolling. After all, they had big plans and were committing big bucks to this partnership.

Time was money, and they knew that better than anyone. They coordinated a call to bridge the ocean and soon convened to discuss the roadmap. The new behemoth partner was crystal clear on the vision, and the priority was to complete their project first.

Tomás knew this to be the case from day one and had no qualms about it. He figured perhaps a few months tops, and the spotlight would then shift to his baby to prepare for its launch to the masses. "No worries, gentlemen. We will get this done. And, it will be perfect!" he told them.

And he had every reason to believe it to be the case. By then, he had years of experience running teams, meeting deadlines, and producing results with far fewer resources. It would be a slam dunk.

Soon after that, they pulled the trigger, and it was off to the races. Once again, Tomás began working diligently and tirelessly. He had no issue despite the time difference, but this time was not disheartened. The project was looking promising. Tomás was also happy with his work and felt good all the way around with the situation. He had been providing regular progress reports with no mention of dissatisfaction.

It was time to reconvene with the top brass. Tomás scheduled the call and eventually anxiously and proudly shared his satisfaction with the team he was assigned and the progress. All and all, a glowing report. "So, gentlemen, we should be done shortly." He concluded.

"We are thrilled to hear about the progress and how well you are working with the team. Well done!" the men praised. "We would like to talk with you about the new research we have received on the project." They informed him.

"Absolutely," Tomás replied. "Again, we very much like your work and progress." They reiterated. "The data we have been collecting as we have been moving along is indicating we should focus on another area. We would like you to abandon the existing plan and shift to a new one. One that we are happy to share with you now." They stated.

Silence! Tomás was speechless! Months of work gone, Wasted and now a delay for the grand finale. Tomás could not have been more perturbed. He was in no position to quarrel. They were funding everything; even if he did not agree with this scenario, they were his distribution channel. His path to financial success, the road to his lifelong dream, was now not at an impasse. It was not easy news to digest. Nevertheless, Tomás maintained a high degree of professionalism, and graciously agreed. "Perhaps a few month's delayed, but I will still have my cake when it's over," he thought.

Tomás informed the team, and they accepted the pivot as if it was all in a day's work. And, for them, it was. They were getting paid by the company to do whatever the company wanted; it was of no consequence to them.

Tomás, on the other hand, had his project on hold, the delay was most disconcerting, and his nerves began to unravel with every week that passed without approval or disapproval. He was concerned that silence would soon signal trouble as it had previously.

That's when I got the call! "Hi Keith, its Mark. I have Tomás on the line may I put him through" "Yes, thanks, buddy!" I replied.

"Hey, Tomás. How are you? What's going on? How was the honeymoon?" It had been some time since we last spoke, and I had assumed he was calling to tell that his invention already launched, and he was on his way to his fortune.

"Oh, Keith, I am okay." Replied a constrained Tomás. The honeymoon was fantastic, and we are still very much in love. Thank you for asking." In a solemn tone. "Tomás, you don't sound well, are you sick?" I inquired. "No, no, I'm in good health. I want a moment of your time if you would be so kind. I don't know who else to talk with Keith." "Sure, Tomás, what's wrong?" And he began to explain the story, his doubts, and reservations. "Keith, what do you think I should do?"

Once again, no one ever seems to call for the easy question! This time I wasn't so fast on my feet and genuinely needed some time. I asked him if I could think about it and get back to him shortly.

"Keith, thank you so much! I'm sorry to bother you!" "Tomás, don't worry, the situation will work out for the best one way or another, no worries. I'll get back to you shortly."

> "No problem can be solved from the same level of consciousness that created it."
>
> ALBERT EINSTEIN

"Tomás' most certainly had a predicament. I listened carefully to his comments and sensed there was more to the story as I reflected on our previous conversations. My intuition was sending me clear signals. I had significant reservations about sharing those thoughts, so I opted to let things simmer.

After all, it had been a long road, and this was not an ideal place to run into trouble. Tomás had expired his capital and had been relying on this partnership. Without them, he was dead in the water with no runway whatsoever. He needed them, and it appeared things were going sideways with them.

With a fair dose of time, the thoughts remained the same, and it was time to call. I promised myself I would try to keep things upbeat, avoid the unpleasantries, and only share the minimum necessary. I knew that the odds at this point we're heavily stacked against Tomás and that less of a conversation would be more.

I wanted him to give it his all, and if it were his Destiny, go down swinging to the end rather than throwing in the towel. I related to his situation, and he knew it. I had shared stories with him of my struggles, and he saw himself as a fighter like me. We had become friends. I wanted to see him succeed and so I was resolved to give him the best advice I could.

"Hey Tomás, I hope today is a better day for you!" Thank you, Keith, Thank you" grateful as always. "Tomas, I've given the situation a great deal of thought, and I will keep the advice very short.

You need to focus on a different strategic partner." One that will license what you have, and this way, you won't need to do anything more. You can tell them that part of the licensing agreement will be that you will complete the technology that is ninety percent complete and stay on for a salary if necessary. Still, they need to pay you upfront and pay a royalty as well something along the lines of say seven to ten percent. That needs to be your focus!

I'm afraid to say, but the people you are dealing with now, most likely are not intending to help you with your invention. And you need to make the deal I'm describing before these people pull the rug out from under you and leave you with nothing. Do you understand?" I emphasized.

"Yes! But I haven't even been able to get my messages returned. It is challenging what you suggest." "Yes, Tomás, it is. But it's your best chance because it's possible!" "Thank you, Keith! Thank you! I think you are correct! Thank you!" and he hung up.

Tomás pressed forward with his partnership and complied with each change order that was issued. It was tedious, time-consuming, and with no visible end in sight. The stress continued to mount every day, and with every new quest. The lack of feedback was not helping either, and he felt that time was slipping away. It no longer appeared to be a partnership to him, and it was as if he had no control over his Destiny. He feverishly continued his outreach for another alternative solution but to no avail.

Tomás finally got a call from the two kind Asian gentlemen. An unannounced call! "Finally! Perhaps some good news?" he thought. It was atypical to receive a call without notice, but perhaps good news needed no introduction?

The two gentlemen he once admired and respected greeted him quickly and immediately expressed their appreciation for his commitment and hard work and praised him for everything he concluded on their behalf. However, they had come to the difficult decision to terminate the partnership and part ways. They wanted nothing more from him, and they wanted nothing to do with his invention.

Tomás had just witnessed the unthinkable! How could they? It was one thing to choose not to proceed with their project, but to summarily reject his invention was insulting and painful to the core. It was not just his invention; it was also his Destiny. He gave them his all, and they merely took advantage of his expertise. It happened just as I had told him it might? How could he not have seen it coming? More importantly, what would become of his invention and his future?

CHAPTER 13

The End of the Line

IT APPEARED THAT TIME had run its course. Tomás was now powerless to reconcile that his Destiny would not materialize. "Where had I gone wrong?" he struggled. He had dreamt about his invention, its impact, and its success in immense detail. The value of what he had to offer, the mass adoption, the change that would come. His new bride, the family he wanted to create, and the promises he had made to Elena, his family, and his friends.

There was nothing left. It was akin to the day I snuck a smoke from my wife's il Bisonti and headed for the stoop in front of my house as my wife and children napped. The only thing left was acceptance and time.

Tomás took inventory of his now meager resources. Tomás did receive compensation from the two gentlemen. However, everything he was able to accumulate above his monthly nut went to the development of his project. There now remained nothing more than a few thousand dollars.

He was now mentally, physically, and financially exhausted and needed some time for himself. It was a defining moment.

Despite the limited cash, he opted for a change of environment, believing it would help to ease the pain, allow him to regroup, and begin to heal? It was an awkward and uncomfortable situation, but he needed distance. And with that, he timidly reached out to extended family back in Europe. They were ecstatic to hear from him and coaxed him to visit. So, he accepted the invitation and made arrangements to visit for a few weeks. His family was genuinely excited at the prospect of spending time with them.

It had been quite some time since his last visit, and now he was merely a few days away from departing. Before he knew it, he boarded the plane. Tomás walked to his seat in the rear and stored his belongings in the compartment above. He ducked down to clear the compartment door and slipped into what appeared to be quite a slender and confined seat next to the window. It would be home for the next eleven hours.

He fastened his seat belt and gazed out the window to watch the aircrew scurry about to prepare the plane for departure. As he surveilled them loading the luggage on to the conveyor belt and the catering truck unloading the food, he sensed that he too had unfinished business; there was still more to this story.

Nevertheless, it was time to let go of his thoughts and prepare for departure. He relaxed back into his seat, took a deep breath in gratitude, closed his eyes, and soon fell off to sleep.

With only an hour left in the flight, he slowly awoke as he identified the bustling beverage cart approaching. "Would you like a beverage, sir?" Asked the stewardess. Still exhausted, he kindly requested a café and readied himself for arrival.

He pondered how best to keep the conversation with his family to a minimum and yet maintain his usual cheery self. It was a difficult task but something he needed to do. He knew they would understand; however, he nevertheless felt uneasy.

He stepped up from his seat, grabbed his bag, and strolled off the jet. He made his way to the baggage claim area and then to customs for a momentary delay as they examined his passport and then waved him on through.

As he exited the terminal, he spotted his relatives nearby and received his greeting quickly with big smiles, hugs, kindness, and love. The kind only family can offer. He felt happy being with them and very much looked forward to the scenic commute to their modest countryside home. They tossed his luggage in the trunk, and off they went.

The excursion was relaxing and hypnotic as they meandered through the rolling green countryside, reminiscing over incidents and folly. The smell of freshly cut grass had permeated the coach, and the cattle seen grazing in the distance. Unbridled quarter horses were galloping free, and there wasn't a single negative thought in the air. It certainly was a mystical place he had once left behind. It was magical, and he was now happy to return.

Within a few hours, they had arrived and showed him to his quarters, leaving him to rest. With dinner only a few hours away, he took them up on the offer and lay down and sealed his eyes.

No sooner than he fell asleep, he had awoken to feel refreshed and energized. Something felt right! He cleaned himself up and made his way to meet everyone for a delicious family dinner.

A voracious greeting and feast embraced him, and the evening carried on. The conversations flourished on family, values, joy, and happiness without ever once touching upon failures or work.

Tomás found it cathartic, timely, and necessary. With a belly full of his favorite dishes and libations, he soon retired for the evening to get his rest. Tomorrow would be a new day.

For the next several days, Tomás would take long walks in the countryside to ease his mind and soul. Hours would pass as he would engage with the local villagers and quaint sporadic roadside merchants along his route. He would stop and chat with them sharing stories of life and love that always included his darling, Elena. There was joy, laughter, tears, and life.

He had followed his desire, his heart, his dreams, and his Destiny, and now with acceptance, he was healing. He had now returned to his true joyous and happy self. He knew things were good, and his wondrous Destiny would eventually arrive as he always envisioned.

Two days before his departure, Tomás thought to visit an old dear family friend. One he had not seen in countless years. They had always remarkably shared marvelous moments. As men do, they discussed their epic and unforgettable adventures, dreams, desires, and more. It was time to reconnect.

Tomás headed to see Eduardo. Eduardo had now become a successful businessman and was inhabiting a beautiful estate where he built a Mediterranean villa overlooking the deep blue sea below.

In front of the villa lay an astonishing azure bottomed free-formed saltwater pool with beautiful cascading waterfalls, lustrous cabanas, and chaise lounges lined around the sprawling grounds. There were also two smaller homes, one for guests and the other for the family that oversaw the property in his absence.

As Tomás arrived, he rolled past the expansive mechanized gates and slowly traveled down the long and winding dirt and gravel road admiring the horses on his way to the main house. He eventually approached the main Villa with a rolling stop and was greeted by the lovely caretaker couple. They had been notified of his visit and made sure to expeditiously escorted him to the pool to reunite him with his dear old friend Eduardo.

It was a bit of a hike along a well-manicured white rock path, but within a handful of minutes, Tomás spotted Eduardo at the far end of the pool. He was dressed in white linen and sported a deep olive tan. Tomás could not mistake him even with years passed.

Tomás shouted out, "Eduardo! How are you, my friend?" Eduardo spotted Tomás and shouted the same. They swiftly narrowed the gap, and when they met each committed to a long and meaningful embrace. After all, they had shared a great deal, even though many years had passed. They patted each other on the backs in an encouraging manner and praised each other before turning to sit poolside on the Venetian chaises.

It was if they had just seen each other yesterday. Tomás and Eduardo picked up their conversation, sharing trials and tribulations. They listened intently and cheered and consoled each other as they exchanged tales. They joked and laughed even over about their serious affairs. And, once Tomás finally settled in and became comfortable, he began to share the story of his invention.

However, no sooner than he started, they were interrupted. "I am most sorry to have to disturb you, Mr.

Eduardo, but I'm afraid this cannot wait. Your presence is necessary at the main house for a phone call." Said the caretaker.

"Tomás, I am sorry, but I am afraid I must attend to this matter. But I promise you I won't be too long." He assured Tomás with a gentle pat on the back. As Eduardo dashed off in his white garb, he glanced back and said with a sparkling smile, "Enjoy the view, it's magical!" And off he went.

Tomás nodded his head in agreement. "Yes, of course, it's magical! Sure, why not?" Enthusiastically! He agreed and then swirled around in opposition to the gentle cool breeze to capture the view. It was magical, energetic, expansive, and invigorating! The feeling that anything was possible overcame him. He could not help but smile and admire the beauty before him. "If only this moment could last forever!" He thought.

In that moment of bliss, Tomás' cell phone sounded. He shook his head and chuckled as he peered downward. He pulled the often-pesky accessory from his left pants pocket. He raised it to his ear and in his typical happy and grateful tone, as he looked out at the view, and answered with a big, "Hello! It's Tomás!"

The voice on the other end replied, "Hello Tomás, my sincere apologies for not getting back to you sooner, please forgive me. Thank you so much for sharing your invention! May I purchase it for $12 Million?"

CHAPTER 14

Mystic Money

WHEN WE WITNESS OTHER people achieve exceptional results, we often get an overwhelming special feeling. Perhaps, an athlete sets a new record. Or, maybe an actor or musician wins an unprecedented number of awards, and on and on and on.

You know what I mean. I'm talking about that goosebumps moment. We have all experienced it, yet brush it off as just excitement.

Could it be more than just an exciting moment? Was it only a moment of chance? Most of the time, the answer is a quick, yes. And, that is because without having to apply any great deal of thought or Consciousness, it's the fastest, most comfortable, and convenient explanation. After all, 90% of all our thoughts are the same as yesterday's, which leaves little room for new ideas to emerge.

However, on the other hand, if we allow new thoughts or Consciousness to emerge or pass through our brains, it is not surprising at all that we see people achieving such fantastic results so frequently. We hear of incredible feats and triumphs every day in the news. These people did the work. Countless hours of work! They didn't just plod along aimlessly either. Surely, there must be more to the story than a simple matter of chance? And there always is!

Over time, as they reflect on the big picture, they somehow gain clarity and account for their good fortune. So, why only in hindsight?

Well, there is always more to the story than merely following the three or four steps to success. It is a process that includes actions and, more critical, observation, adjustment, and more. As people pass through the process that leads them to their success, they are busy doing and often not spending time being, observing, and documenting their journey.

It is with the time we are all fortunate enough to be allowed to distance ourselves from the constant challenges and observe them more objectively, thereby providing more accurate accounts. These observations and instances are what become invaluable and are often what astute scholars seek to facilitate or shorten their journey.

In other words, there is tremendous value in other people's experiences or processes if they routinely lead to replicable results. Don't you want to know the proven way to achieve a great result time and time again?

Of course, you do! Finding ways to shortcut our way to great results is why we follow other people on social media, read or listen to books, listen to a podcast, and so forth so that we may study others to glean shortcuts for our challenges. And, it all makes perfectly good sense.

In the case of Michael Jordan, through reflection, Michael made it clear that there was no simple three or four-step process to transform him into a super athlete. Simply standing on a court and throwing the ball more times at the hoop was not going to be enough for him to improve enough to make it to the pros.

He was aware, or Conscious, and knew there was much more required to become a better basketball player, let alone a stellar player. He talked about how he viewed every obstacle as a strength rather than a weakness and how he especially valued other's negative comments and input since it merely increased is the internal motivation to strive for even more significant achievements. It illustrates his unique Point of View (POV) and mindset. These two components are vital to every process and for achieving success.

With this in mind, let's take a closer look at the strategy or formula and the process Tomás implemented to achieve success. Remember, achieving Success requires more than just doing work. It requires a Plan, Values, coordinated efforts, and more. We commonly refer to how we pass through this collectively as the "Process." Once I unveil the Formula and walk you through the process, you will then be able to apply them together to your thoughts and desires to pursue and achieve your objectives, goals, dreams, and success.

If we look back at my early encounters with Tomás, we know that he had the thought or Consciousness to develop and deliver something of value to many people to affect their lives. His invention, as he called it, was explicitly designed to allow people to capture more with far less effort. It was his proposition.

Additionally, he was also providing everyone with a much better user experience, which collectively would change people's lives. Yes, Tomás most certainly gave his venture a great deal of thought because he was aware or conscious that it would take a considerable amount of expertise and time to create and deliver the invention and to become successful with it.

His Desire to achieve his goal was straightforward. He wanted to provide value and change lives so that he may personally experience happiness and reap other material rewards.

The idea of obtaining satisfaction and rewards was his Motivation. As discussed earlier, happiness is an internal motivational force as opposed to material rewards, which are an external force. Because his primary motivation was internal, it gave him that additional leverage to plow through the most difficult challenges with Action and not throw in the towel.

When it came to living up to his Values and his perceived Destiny, there would be no compromising. Paramount was his true Belief that this would make his life complete. Yet, had it been solely to acquire money, he very likely would have given up much sooner with the belief that the challenges were just not worth the reward.

Similar to Michael Jordan, Tomás encountered resistance and obstacles as he progressed that left him seriously challenged and stressed. Like any skillful entrepreneur or athlete, he asserted his focus on his determination to prevail.

More importantly, he maintained an open mind and chose to focus on finding better solutions. To do so, it required having the presence to realize the situation was moving beyond himself. It was time for another pair of eyes to survey the big picture better. So, prudently he reached out for assistance, advice, and guidance. This process continued repeatedly and unending as he reevaluated his Plan at each juncture where the resistance became intolerable.

Each new pair of eyes brought a new perspective or Point of View (POV) and a unique opportunity. Tomás was then able to form better conclusions and implement adjustments, if and when necessary, to reduce resistance yet remain consistent with his Desire, Motivation, Beliefs, Values, and achieving his Destiny. It is known as "Alignment" and is a critical component of the process of Success.

Think of alignment as the grease that keeps the wheels turning smoothly. Without alignment or a lubricant, there is friction. This friction produces heat, and as the quantity of movement increases, so does the amount of heat making the situation more untenable and providing the type of environment where things melt before you. Accordingly, Alignment is critical for keeping things together, minimizing resistance, and for maintaining the necessary momentum to achieve Success.

There are always, and always will be, those who write off remarkable moments and achievements to chance because they are too busy or uninterested in understanding how others achieved success. However, for those who chose to inquire about other people's remarkable results and triumph, they are pleasantly surprised to glean the unique commonality of Alignment. Almost all accounts of these feats include moments of effortlessness. A state of perfection frequently described as surreal or hypnotic, and that is precisely why these people cross the finish line is because of this Alignment or flow.

CHAPTER 15

Mapping & Mastering Your Success

IN THIS CHAPTER, WE will identify and discuss the steps necessary to get you set up for success. While it would be nice to validate that there are just a handful of steps to achieve success, that would be merely perpetuating only one of the many falsehoods that permeate society.

Yes, many people are just looking for a quick fix with a few steps, but we can see from very successful people, real Success requires considerably more than only a few steps and work. It requires mastering a Process.

Whether we are talking about Michael Jordan, Lady Gaga, Jeff Bezos, Mahatma Gandhi, or Great Thunberg, to achieve meaningful results, they all had to master their Process. And, in this chapter, you will learn how to master yours.

First, we will sequentially address the steps, like a straight line. A straight line between two points is the most efficient way to get from one place to another and makes good sense.

However, it is essential to note that since not everyone views or experiences things in quite the same way. If for any reason, the steps do not seem to appear in order, it is perfectly fine and does not mean that you cannot achieve your desired outcome. It merely means that your view is slightly different. Nevertheless, provided you apply the correct Process outlined, you may still be able to achieve your desired results.

Second, we will discuss the overarching concepts that affect and complement the steps and how to apply them to produce your Process for Success. It is an ongoing process that requires observation, reflection, and adjustments. Therefore, I highly recommend documenting your impressions and corrections because you will most certainly need to revisit them as you encounter sticking or friction points. Also, taking written notes will help to reinforce the observations, adjustments, and keep you focused instead of being disorganized or confused and meandering off course.

As I previously mentioned, the Process includes a systematic method to check and re-check your Process for flaws. You will do this through a series of questions specifically designed to identify the weak spots. Since we have already discussed the steps utilizing Michael and Tomás, it will all be familiar, reasonably simple to follow, and easy to create your roadmap to success.

The necessary steps are the following and appear in sequential order:

1. Thought/Idea
2. Desire
3. Motivation
4. Belief
5. Values
6. Plan
7. Action
8. Destiny/Success

Again, should the steps not be in quite the order you envision, do not be panicked or concerned.

Thought or Idea

To begin, you must have a Thought or an Idea about something you would like to achieve or experience. Perhaps it's a business goal such as create a particular type of business, increase your existing sales to a certain amount, expand your number of employees, go global, or even become number one in your industry.

You may also want to do something personally for yourself, such as travel Europe, improve your golf game, hike Mt. Everest or make a movie. It's your list, so start with the things that you feel most excited about experiencing. The things that we call bucket list items.

Meaning, given a chance, you would want to experience or achieve these things sometime before you leave this planet.

Make a list of your "Top Six Thoughts or Ideas" below:

1. _____

2. _____

3. _____

4. _____

5. _____

6. _____

Desire

Congratulations, you now have your "Top Six" list of the things you Desire! Now, it is time to ruminate on these thoughts or ideas. There is no rush, and the more time you take, the better. You are looking for feelings that validate whether or not you genuinely want these things. Ask yourself, "Why do I want this?" "How does it make me feel when I think about achieving it?" and "On a scale of 1-10, how strong is my Desire to achieve it?" Keep the answers as brief as possible!

	Why?	How?	Scale 1-10
1			
2			
3			
4			
5			
6			

Motivation

Now that you have answered the why question, we now know your Motivation. Is it internal or external Motivation? The answer to this question is critical. Remember, external motivation, such as rewards, will only get you so far. If your Motivation is external, then you may want to consider whether or not you even want to pursue it because the journey may not be worth the reward. If your Motivation is internal, then at least you know you genuinely Desire it, which is vital for the next step, Belief.

Belief

We hear about belief systems or a set of principles or tenets which together form the basis of religion, philosophy, or moral code quite often and with good reason. As I am sure you gleaned from my journey, Michael's and Tomás', we all firmly believed that what we were pursuing was very much attainable. Whether or not others thought it achievable was not one of our considerations. As you can see, the three of us would not give up on our Belief and ultimately achieved what we sought.

This tenet of Belief is one of the single most significant factors of whether or not one prevails in achieving their Success. Just think about how your Belief can alter outcomes.

I'm sure you have been in a situation where you wanted to go to the movies or a store that was nearing its closing hour. You debated back and forth and, at some point, realized you may not even make it to the movie or store in time, and by the time you were ready to decide you realized it was already too late because you either missed the beginning of the movie or the store closed. Of course, you have! We all have, and it's just a small reminder of how our Belief affects our everyday lives.

Accordingly, if you want to achieve your "Top Six," you will need to have the Belief that you can obtain them wholeheartedly. Anything short of your true Belief in attainment will most likely fail. I cannot stress this enough! Your Belief is crucial because it will support your Desire and Motivation, and your lack of it will only allow your Motivation to wane. Therefore, you must be brutally honest with yourself when you ask yourself if it is within you to achieve that which you seek.

Values

Akin to Belief is Values or one's judgment of the things that are important in life. If you perceive and believe that something is so important to your life, then that alone will provide the kind of Motivation for you to accomplish something remarkable. Hence, your Values collectively support your Desire, Belief, and Motivation.

Think of having the Values of living a healthy and lengthy life. If you have this Belief and need to honor this value, then you will have the motivation to exercise and eat appropriately to achieve a healthy and lengthy life that you Desire.

Plan

You've now already established the "Top Six" things you would like to achieve. You have also asked the questions to determine if you have the Desire, Motivation, Belief, and Values necessary for you to Succeed. It is now time to develop your Plan.

Creating your roadmap to Success will require you to define the result. Once you have determined this, such as earn $10,000,000 in ten years or sell the business for $15,000,000 in five years, etc. you may then work backward to determine the benchmarks you will need to hit along the way.

For instance, if you want to earn $10,000,000 over the next ten years, that is roughly $1,000,000 per year. You will then need to determine if you can bring in the $1,000,000 per year or if you are better suited to make it in increasing amounts overtime to get to the goal and what those amounts may be.

Once again, this Plan must be within your Belief and Values for you to achieve it. It requires you to create your custom Plan, and you will need to do a considerable amount of work. The more thorough and well thought out your Plan, the easier it will be to execute it, and the higher the probability you will achieve Success. We will address more on your Plan later in the chapter.

Action

The final step before reaching Success or your Destiny is Action. It is the step where you finally get to find out if your efforts will indeed pay off. From the three accounts I have already provided, you can see that it certainly wasn't smooth sailing for anyone.

However, you do have three examples of achieving Success to meet Destiny. You know what is possible, and just because the three accounts you learned about may have been arduous doesn't mean that it may be the case for you. Remember, you now have a distinct advantage because you now have the steps you need, and once we discuss the correct Process, anything will be possible.

To briefly review, the steps to Success are the following:

1. Thought/Idea
2. Desire
3. Motivation
4. Belief
5. Values
6. Plan
7. Action
8. Destiny/Success

With these in mind, we can address the Process, which includes the other components necessary to Achieve Success. Think of these components as the lubricants that will keep everything moving as you progress towards Success. Without them, the Process will either be extended, stall, or even fall apart.

Alignment

Alignment is the arrangement in a straight line or correct or appropriate relative positions. We systematically discussed the eight steps to Success. As I previously mentioned, even if you approach them in a slightly different order, you will achieve the same result provided you maintain them in Alignment.

In other words, so long as you have a Thought or Idea along with the equivalent Desire, Motivation, Belief, and Values, you will be on your course to achieve your Destiny or Success. Contrary, if, for some reason, you lose your full

Belief that you will achieve success, you will then experience resistance or friction that will either slow you down or cause you to quit.

Similarly, if you decide that you had a change of heart because your Values suddenly changed, you will perhaps no longer possess the same level of Desire or Motivation than when you began resulting in resistance or you giving up on your quest. Or, if your Plan or Action is not in sync with your other steps, you will also experience resistance or friction that could eventually lead to failure.

Alignment, without question, is a critical component to any Process and determines the degree of difficulty one will experience along the way. Therefore, it is imperative to take time to get your steps in Alignment as best as possible before commencing.

Consciousness

Consciousness is the state of being awake and aware of one's surroundings. We often hear this word more often than perhaps we would like? Frequently, it is associated with religious or spiritual beliefs. However, in this context, it is strictly limited to merely being Aware. Therefore, I will refer to either the word Aware or Awareness to be synonymous with Consciousness.

Just as Alignment is so important, so is Awareness. Rigidity in any Plan runs the severe risk of failure. We live in a dynamic world rather than static. Therefore, it is imperative to timely spot transitions in the landscape to be able to adapt and conform to new situations and maintain the Course to Success.

Without the requisite Awareness, we may miss the opportunity to transition, Plans become obsolete, challenges become increasingly more complicated, and you soon tire and even fail. Maintaining your awareness will allow you to monitor the landscape, procure assistance if determined necessary, make adjusts as needed, and stay the course to Success.

Point of View

Point of View or, more commonly referred to as POV, is a particular attitude or way of considering a matter or situation. It is the final element to the Process, and when coupled with Consciousness or Awareness, the two become incalculable factors. They walk hand in hand and provide vital information. Think of them as your vision and your sixth sense, respectively.

First, your Awareness furnishes the ability to notice subtleties, reactions, and changes as you are taking Action according to your Plan. Think of it as an invaluable survey used to manipulate or improve upon your Plan.

Second, increased Awareness facilitates more POVs, which supply additional insights on your Plan and Actions. These insights may then offer more exceptional options for the challenges that may arise along the way.

The following diagram represents the eight steps and the three elements that collectively constitute the Process to achieve Success.

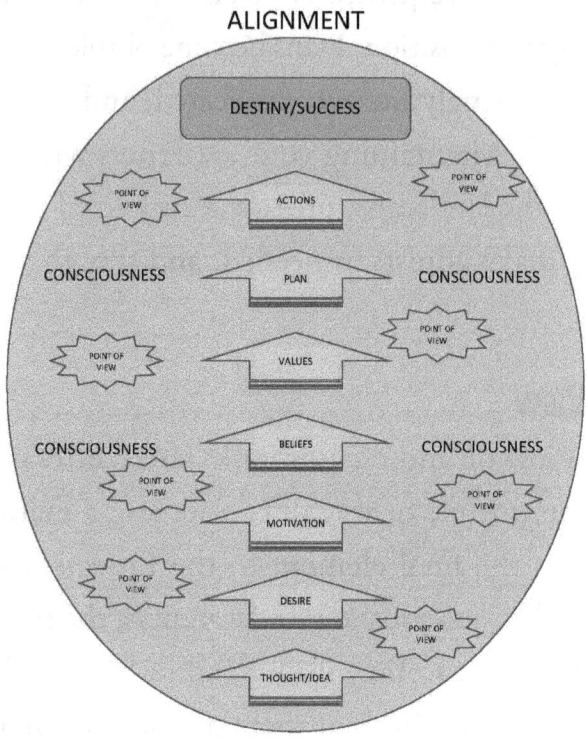

The objective is to maintain Alignment between your Thought or Idea, Desire, Motivation, Beliefs, Values, Plan, and Action to reach your Destiny or Success. Concurrently, maintaining your Consciousness or Awareness of what is transpiring is essential. By doing so, you will be able to see other Points of View from different vantage points. These vantage points will offer additional solutions to the challenges you encounter along the way, making it much more plausible to achieve Success.

CHAPTER 16

Conclusion

INCREDIBLE AND EVEN LIFE-CHANGING thoughts and ideas are seen and published every day, and yet they are routinely unnoticed or dismissed. Without examining the steps and the Process, one never truly never knows of their likelihood of Success. It is only upon further examination, investigation, or reflection that we become aware of why so many of them fail, and so few prevail.

In my case, I was driven by a distinct Belief that my Destiny would be to achieve what most would describe as the "Great American Dream" by the time I was 40. Most would agree that it is a worthy goal yet very ambitious or even unrealistic by the age of 40. I was fortunate to achieve my goal, but I feel even more blessed to learn the steps and Process to Success.

Admittedly, like myself and most, Michael Jordan chose to focus on his goals rather than the psychology behind his journey. It is the most common of choices in the absence of the knowledge to the clear path to Success and the only reasonable option. Yet, with reflection, he, too, gained clarity and insight and now routinely shares the finer details of his journey to uber Success.

In the case of Tomás, the Inventor, we saw how an unassuming shoebox stuffed with old receipts, stale checkbooks, and crumpled documents transformed into a $12,000,000 payday. Similar to other inexperienced entrepreneurs, athletes, actors, etc., Tomás found himself challenged with maintaining Alignment as he also struggled to become a businessman and finding his Process. Despite his business inexperience and the countless challenges, to his credit, he utilized his Awareness and ingenuity to see other Points of View and find solutions to propel him to success.

As you move forward to achieve your Success, keep in mind the importance of both maintaining your Alignment, as illustrated in the diagram above. And, to also remain Conscious or Aware as you routinely question your Belief and Values for reasonableness and your Plan and Action for effectiveness and efficiency as you experience resistance or friction in your Process. Remember, implementing your Consciousness and continuously considering other Points of View to make adjustments as necessary will ultimately be the grease for a smooth journey. Rest assured, with the elements and Process to Success at your fingertips; you will no longer need to rely upon luck.

I look forward to hearing about your Success!

www.ingramcontent.com/pod-product-compliance
Lightning Source LLC
Chambersburg PA
CBHW060530100426
42743CB00009B/1477